# GENESIS
## IN *Poetry*

Jeffrey M Cohen

ISBN 978-0-946000-05-0

Published by: J M Cohen
Ph/fax: 0208 457 5849
jeffreyandgloria@yahoo.co.uk

Typesetting by FiSH Books, Enfield, Middlesex
Printed in Great Britain by Good News Digital Books, Ongar

# CONTENTS

About the author and his work     vii

Introduction     xi

### GENESIS IN POETRY

Creation     1

Adam     5

Eve     9

The Garden of Eden     11

Lilith and the Serpent     14

Eating of the forbidden fruit     16

Cain and Abel     21

Noah and the Ark     26

Life in the Ark     31

'Testing the Waters'     33

Noah's last days     35

Tower of Babel     36

Abram discovers God     39

Abram and The Promised Land     44

Sarai in peril     46

Abram and Lot     48

Wars of the Kings                                   50

Sarai and Hagar                                     52

Circumcision and a name-change                      55

Visit of the three angels                           56

Sodom and Gomorrah                                  58

Lot and the destruction of the cities               61

Lot and his daughters                               63

Isaac and Ishmael                                   64

Binding of Isaac                                    67

Death and burial of Sarah                           71

Purchase of the Cave of Machpelah                   72

A wife for Isaac                                     75

Jacob and Esau                                      81

Purchase of the birthright                          83

Isaac in adversity and posterity                    85

Jacob, Esau and the birthright                      88

The dream of the ladder                             97

Approaching Laban's home                            99

Jacob at Laban's home                              101

Reuben and the mandrakes                           105

Farewell to Laban's home                           107

Jacob and Esau's reunion                           112

Wrestling with the angel                           114

The Jacob-Esau encounter                           116

Dinah                                              117

Death of Rachel                                    122

Reuben and Bilhah                                  123

Joseph                                             125

Joseph's dreams                                    128

Kidnapping and sale of Joseph                      129

Judah and Tamar                                    133

Joseph in Egypt                                    137

The butler and the baker                           140

Pharaoh's dreams                                   142

Joseph's rise to power                             146

Reunion of Joseph and his brothers                 149

Allegations of espionage!                          150

A ruse to bring Benjamin to Egypt                  153

Further trials for the brothers                    155

Joseph discloses his identity                      158

Jacob and family settle in Egypt                   160

Jacob's last days                                  163

Jacob's deathbed blessing                          165

Death and burial of Jacob                          168

The brothers' apprehension                         170

Joseph's final farewell                            171


NOTES TO THE TEXT                                  173

To Gloria
With love and gratitude

And to our children

Harvey and Lorraine
Suzanne and Keith
Judith and Bobby
Lewis and Suzanne

And to our adorable grandchildren –
Poetry in motion

Joel, Phil, Alex, Eliot, Abigail,
Charlotte, Ariel, Maddy, Sasha,
Zack, Leo, Solly, Jake & Maisie

# ABOUT THE AUTHOR
# AND HIS WORK

Jeffrey M Cohen retired four years ago as rabbi of the largest Orthodox congregation in the UK. He has also served as lecturer at the universities of London and Glasgow, and is the author of 20 books and over 200 articles on aspects of Biblical interpretation and Jewish theology. He has also contributed many popular articles for the Jewish press. A list of his publications is available on his website at rabbijeffrey.co.uk

He has always enjoyed writing poetry, but it was a holiday in the English Lake Districts, in the summer of 2008, when following the Wordsworth trail, that inspired him to write this poetic novel, incorporating all the main episodes of the biblical book of Genesis. His primary objective was to bring the Bible to life as an inspirational and engaging story to a contemporary generation that, in the main, has ceased reading it.

He chose the rhyming poetic genre in order to enliven the subject matter, given that, although the stories themselves are fascinating and full of pathos, yet most of the standard translations are written in prosaic and archaic language. Since those biblical stories of the domestic lives, loves and rivalries of the founding fathers of mankind are generally presented in a rather sketchy form, omitting essential background details, such as behavioural motivation, emotional responses, and the supplementary narrative that must have accompanied many of the situations, the author realised that a great deal of explanatory material had to be woven into his narrative if it was to leave the reader satisfied and fully engaged.

Among the sources he utilises, apart from his own poetic imagination, are the ancient and medieval writings with which, as a Jewish Bible scholar, he is familiar, such as post-biblical and folkloristic (Midrashic) expositional writings. Although these are, primarily, Jewish traditions, they would have been known by both Jews and Christians in the early centuries C.E. A large number of such traditions subsequently found their way into the Koran. A work such as this, which weaves them into the biblical narrative, should commend itself, therefore, to those of any faith who have an interest in, and love for, the Bible.

Since completing this project, Jeffrey Cohen has presented selections of it on the radio, to schools and to literary groups. The responses were consistently enthusiastic, as demonstrated by the following sample audience reviews:

Thank you for sending me Genesis in Poetry. I have enjoyed reading it. In fact I was greatly tempted to sing parts of it, though I resisted. The close rhymes and steady rhythm are indeed very musical, and I wonder if you have considered setting at least a section of it to music?

(Ann Sansom, proprietor of The Poetry Business, and editor and director of The North Magazine (see //www.annsansom.co.uk)

★ ★ ★

Thank you so much for reading extracts from your poetic version of Genesis. I do congratulate you upon the vitality and range of feeling you achieve in your use of couplet. The lines Chamor speaks, in smooth, assured and superficial tones, in your telling of the story make this heartless and powerful figure as vivid as Claudius celebrating his assumption of Denmark's throne at the opening of "Hamlet".

Mr Philip Skelker, Head Master, Immanuel College, Bushey, And former teacher of English at Eton.

★ ★ ★

Thank you for your wonderful Genesis in Poetry evening. People are still talking about it as an unforgettable experience, which was not just absorbingly enjoyable, but had your audience totally captivated. Among the audience acclamations I heard were, 'brilliant' 'highly original and refreshing' 'inspiring', 'intriguing and provocative.' Your own recitation added to the pleasure of the imaginative verse. If schools presented the subject in that way, there would be far more enthusiastic students around!

Naomi West, Former teacher and organiser of poetry reading
in aid of Laniado Hospital, Netanya

★ ★ ★

Your lecture and poetry were by any standards, masterly and deserve a wider but not necessarily Jewish audience. Jeanette and I found your performance (excuse the word but it had a media feel) educational, intellectually stimulating and entertaining – no mean feat!

Raymond Cannon, Former Chair of Governors, JFS, London

★ ★ ★

This book is a joy to read out loud and to listen to. Each section vivifies the experiences of our forebears and brings people together in animated discussion.

Yvonne Green, Poet

# INTRODUCTION
## *Rhyming Poetry*

I am well aware that poetry is a subjective matter, and that a poem that one person loves may well leave another totally unmoved. Although modern poetry has largely liberated itself from the constraints of metre and rhyme, that did not deter me from employing them in this work, because I regarded them as most suited to the style of the biblical subject matter I was re-telling. The great popularity of Pam Ayres remains undiminished, notwithstanding that the poetry establishment looks askance at her employment of poems that scan and rhyme. I was also encouraged by a comment of the contemporary poet, William Radice:

> 'Freer forms can be appropriate for some purposes, and, as T. S. Elliot said: "No verse is free for the man who wants to do a good job." But poets who want to catch a particular mood or write a poem to suit a person or occasion need the maximum number of arrows in their quiver. To be unable to use traditional forms or create adventurous new ones reduces the chances of a bull's eye' (*The Times*, Jan 13th 2009, p. 24).

That there is still a place for metre and rhyme may also be demonstrated by the fact that, as I write, a play, entitled *La Bête* (The Beast), and written entirely in rhyming couplets, has just opened on the London stage to rave reviews. Libby Purves writes that 'the comic rhymes were brilliantly delivered from the start' (The Times, July 8th 2010).

## *Objective of the Work*

I am not insensitive to the fact that, in the eyes of many traditionalists, any attempt to paraphrase the Bible – the most sublime and incomparable spiritual and literary composition – would be deemed facetious . The Bible is, indeed, the heritage of mankind, and has thus made a unique contribution not only to the latter's religious, ethical and moral perceptions but also to its cultural, linguistic and aesthetic development and appreciation. Let me state categorically, therefore, that I am not offering my version as a replacement for the original, but rather as an attempt to stimulate further interest in it. It is directed especially (though not exclusively) toward a younger generation that may be under the mistaken impression that the Biblical narrative cannot compare in interest, power and inspiration with such modern literary classics as *Harry Potter* or *The Lord of the Rings*. My objective is, therefore, to rekindle interest so that my readers may be encouraged to proceed to the original Biblical text in order to (re)acquaint themselves with it and study it in greater detail.

I have attempted to re-write Genesis in a poetic form, with a light, and, where appropriate, whimsical, touch. Episodes are expanded by the inclusion of ideas or traditions borrowed from post-biblical Jewish sources, both expositional and folkloristic, and from my own imagination as I have attempted to transport myself back into the biblical situation. I have also attempted to fill in some background, resolve some of the many difficulties in the text, provide causation or elucidation where this is missing, and, in general, produce an absorbing and lyrical version for those for whom the translations are too challenging.

I am, of course, fully aware that there is nothing inherently novel in this genre. A well-known British actor and author, David Kossoff (d. 2005), delighted radio and theatre audiences with his free prose renderings of the biblical stories. But time has moved on, and the Bible is not as pivotal, authoritative or popular in most countries as it once was.

But centuries before Kossoff, in John Milton's immortal dramatic poem, *Samson Agonistes,* published 1671, we have a rendering of the famous biblical episode of Judges chs. 13-16. Milton's approach was to attempt to portray the inner mental torment and emotional struggle – the agony/agonistes – experienced by the betrayed, blinded and tormented Samson, rather than to provide a mere re-telling of the episode.

In 1825, Byron published thirteen poems on biblical themes, though they were all based on the later books, rather than the Pentateuch. He undertook that assignment in response to a request by a Jewish musician, Isaac Nathan, that he produce lyrics rooted in biblical themes that might serve as an accompaniment to Nathan's own music.

But the idea of paraphrasing and expanding upon the biblical narrative stretches back into antiquity. In the centuries immediately preceding the turn of the Common Era, the Reading of the Law in synagogue in Israel was accompanied by a *Targum*, a verse-by-verse, Aramaic translation. This was recited for the benefit of the Aramaic-speaking, uneducated masses who did not comprehend the Classical Hebrew of Holy Writ. Some versions of that *Targum* are quite expansive, containing Midrashic (expositional and folkloristic) elements revealing the primary objective of those official translators. That was to bring the text to life for the worshippers by offering background supplement and paraphrase, rather than mere translation, and to arouse and engage the interest of the reader by the inclusion of fascinating legendary and exotic ideas. The present work may be viewed as following in that spirit.

The ancient rabbis of the Talmud (1st–7th century CE) had a maxim that 'Words of Holy Writ are poor in one context and wealthy in another.' By that they meant that some episodes are extremely wordy, partaking of seemingly unnecessary repetition of already recorded material (Such as the repetition by Eliezer, servant of Abraham, on his arrival at the home of Laban, of all his experiences and conversations during the course of his journey there to find a wife for Isaac. See Genesis ch.24). Other episodes, by contrast, are described in the barest of outline. Hence, using their finely-honed spirituality, profound moral and ethical sensibility and supremely romantic and poetic imagination, those sages set themselves the task of attempting to supplement the Biblical narrative wherever it was lacking in 'wealth,' and bringing into sharper focus the character and personality of its heroes and rogues, saints and sinners.

## The dramatic imagination

It will be instructive to refer to a few examples of situations that called for the employment of the dramatic imagination. A very lengthy description is given by the Torah to the episode of the making of Noah's ark and the saving of Noah and his family. We are told that the animals came in two by two, but nowhere is there any attempt to name the animals or to describe their diet, the particular time of the day or night that each of them preferred to eat or the demands that they made on poor Noah. These aspects of the situation a zoologist, a social historian, a child, and certainly a poet would wish to consider. The Torah left it entirely to us to do so.

Early Biblical Hebrew expresses itself in rather general and concrete terms. It did not develop the vocabulary to describe detailed and nuanced emotions, Take the Hebrew verb *a-ha-v*, for example. It suffices to convey a whole range of emotions: First, 'to love' – as in the case of the passionate love of a man and a woman. Secondly, 'to engage spiritually and emotionally' in a non-amorous relationship – as in, 'You shall love (*Ve'ahavta*) the Lord your God'; and, thirdly, 'profound emotional concern' – as in 'You shall love (*Ve'ahavta*) your neighbour as yourself". The illustrious scholar and patriarch of ancient Israel, Hillel, accurately put his finger on the impossibility of defining the precise nuance of *a-ha-v* in this latter verse when he resorted to rendering the phrase negatively, as, 'What is hateful to you, do not unto your neighbour'.

So we have one single verb representing the entire gamut of disparate emotions, from social concern, on the one hand, to passionate love, on the other. Hence, again, the poet is entitled to attempt to define and describe the deeper and broader emotions that might underlie such biblical generality, and to seek to re-tell a particular episode, embodying those perspectives. We may conjecture that that is the form the Torah might well have employed had it set out to provide more than the shortest digest of Israel's early history.

Then again, take the account of the night-long struggle of Jacob with the shadowy heavenly being (Genesis 32:25ff.). The text states merely that, 'a man wrestled with him until dawn,' but the identity of that 'man' is shrouded in mystery. Aside from the biblical commentator, the poet and the artist are also keenly interested in the nature of that struggle: Was it real, symbolic, or in a dream? Whichever of these, the imagination is eager to depict the nature of the adversary and the pugilistic spirit of the encounter.

We can but speculate on what faith in God might have been fostered, and what atheism might have been prevented, had the biblical text included the astronomical data and chemical equations that God employed in the act of Creation. More is concealed than revealed. But it is the task and passionate desire of the philosophers by means of their logical deduction, the poets by means of their imagination, and commentators by means of their mastery of the textual implications and knowledge of the history and archaeology of the ancient Near-East, to attempt to fill in those many lacunae.

The Torah devotes a mere nine verses to the episode of the Tower of Babel, though, again, the rich literature of the Midrash amply compensates for that. The poet's imagination is inevitably aroused to discover more of the tension that would have suffused that situation – the first wholesale rebellion against God. Obviously in that context, as in most of the others I treat, it is the Midrashic perspectives that provide the inspirational starting-points.

## The Midrashic genre

A notable example of my Midrashic borrowing is in my account of the story of the creation of both the universe and man. I have relied on the tradition of the angels' strong opposition to God's plan to create morally-weak and rebellious humans, and, secondly, the idea that God created and destroyed several prototypes or experimental worlds before satisfying himself that ours was the one he would sustain. I depict God as revealing this fact to Adam, as a warning to him to ensure that he and his posterity justified their and the world's existence. I envisage Adam as desperate to know whether or not his offspring would, indeed, satisfy that divine prerequisite or whether they would also be consigned to oblivion. This creates a very fraught and dramatic encounter, in the spirit of the desperate negotiation that Abraham conducted with God in order to save the righteous of Sodom.

For students and adults who are familiar with the episodes of the book of Genesis, my poetry will not be required in order to discharge the function of an educational tool. I hope that it will be enjoyed, however, as a form of religious entertainment, or, more accurately, as a Midrash, which also set out to discharge that function.

The sages who created the Midrashic genre could never have dreamt that those fruits of their creative spiritual imagination would ever be perceived as historical reality or as representing the Torah's literal sense, yet the religious fundamentalist position has had no trouble believing precisely that. In truth, those early sages dreamed themselves back into the biblical events in order to provide missing background information, motivation, personality and character delineation. Often, the core motivation of their expositions was also to provide a nationalistic rallying call in the face of the depression that must have gripped the nation as a result of Rome's tightening grip. Another motivation was to offer religious guidance as to Orthodox belief in the struggle against idolatry and heresy. And finally, their expositions enabled them to mine timely moral lessons from the text.

Because Midrash is a rich tapestry of personal ideas and creativity, it is rare to find just one interpretation. Indeed, more frequently, sages offer variant or even opposing interpretations. Thus, on the verse, 'And God place a sign upon Cain (4:15), we find widely differing suggestions as to the nature of that special sign, with one sage actually deriding the suggestion of another:

Rabbi Judah said: The sign was that God caused the bright rays of the sun to permanently shine on him. R. Nehemiah retorted: Do you really think that the Holy One would possibly cause his sun to shine on such a wicked man? No, the implication is that God caused leprosy to break out on him. Rav said: God provided him with a dog for his protection. Abba Joseph said: He caused a horn to sprout forth from his forehead.

Each sage was clearly expressing his own spiritual speculation. And that is Midrash. Not surprisingly, the Midrashic sages themselves adopted the principle that 'we must not be too critical when it comes to Midrashic expositions.' By that they meant that we should not be surprised if the ideas expounded cannot be harmonised with the text or with each other, or if they appear to challenge history, chronology or even logic. And it is with this in mind that I justify having had the temerity to dip in, at random, to the Midrash's spiritual paint-box, and to select and mix some of its most brilliant and iridescent colours as and when required for my own poetic tapestry and imagination.

## Poetry of the Bible

The original Hebrew style of the Book of Genesis – and, for that matter, the rest of the Bible – cannot be described as that of 'every-day language'. It was written in a unique, classical, literary style, employing grammatical and syntactical forms that are confined to the literary genre. Even the ostensibly prose passages possess a rhythmic poetic quality. Indeed, a selection from the Pentateuch, or Five Books of Moses, is 'chanted' in synagogues each week, and the text of a Hebrew Bible is also accompanied by the musical symbols or notations, above or below each word. In addition, so many books of the Bible were written at the outset in poetic form, chiefly the books of Psalms, Proverbs and Job, as well as the prophecies of the great prophets, Isaiah, Jeremiah and Ezekiel, the Minor Prophets and three of the five Megilloth (Scrolls), namely, *Shir Hashirim* (Song of Songs), *Eikhah* (Lamentations) and *Kohelet* (Ecclesiastes). Their phraseology is lyrical, in its basic meaning of words fit to be sung to the accompaniment of the lyre, the most popular musical instrument of biblical times, and it partakes of a conciseness – often conveying a complex idea in three or four words – that no translation can match.

Well into the Midrashic era, from the 6th century CE. onward, poetic expression was more finely honed, and a new and distinctive genre of religious poetry was created, in Israel, by sages, masters of the Bible and Midrash, such as Yosi ben Yosi, Yannai and Kalir. Their work went by the name *piyyut*, borrowed from the Greek word, *poetas* ('poetry'), and was written as a supplement and inspirational commentary to the main kernel of the service.

In the course of time those liturgical poems became so popular that they gained the status of prayer in their own right, entering the daily, Sabbath and festival prayer books to constitute a major element of the liturgy. If we add to that the large number of psalms that grace our prayers, constituting almost half the content of the daily and Sabbath morning services, we have a very clear idea of the importance that rabbinic tradition placed on the poetic genre. Indeed, most of the authors of sacred poetry were themselves rabbis. Poetry, for them, was the supreme means of spiritual expression, and a unique vehicle of transcendence.

And it is in that spirit that this poetry is offered. If, by simplifying the narratives, and synthesizing the creative imagination of those spiritually-intoxicated authors of Midrash and folklore, I have made them more accessible, and increased interest in the study of the Bible, then I shall assuredly be forgiven for having had the temerity to pursue this non-traditional approach.

## *A novel approach to Bible study?*

*Genesis in Poetry* sets out to provide biblical knowledge to those who have only a passing acquaintance with its narrative or who have forgotten its details, as well as inspiration and entertainment to those who have already read and studied it.

As will become apparent from my Notes to the Text, with its numerous references to the Midrashic and Talmudic sources, as well as to the insights of medieval and modern commentaries that have provided the inspiration for my ideas, this work is also intended as an educational tool. For this reason I have frequently drawn attention to wider issues that flow from particular episodes or elements within it. It is perhaps my (over-ambitious?) hope, therefore, that this work might provide a helpful and interesting introduction to the biblical narrative.

In conclusion, I offer sincere thanks to those who have encouraged this project from the outset, and offered much-welcomed help, advice and criticism. These include my adored wife, Gloria, who also read the proofs, the poet Yvonne Green, Mr Stewart Cass of Vallentine Mitchell Publishers, Mr Adam Arnold who kindly provided the book cover, Mrs Daphne Band and other close friends in Netanya and London, and Mr Philip Skelker, Head Master of Immanuel College, Bushey.

**JMC**

# GENESIS IN POETRY

## by Jeffrey M Cohen

### Creation

(Genesis 1:1–2:6)

Why just now,
Indeed, why ever,
Infinity's thread
Did God choose to sever?

Whatever possessed him to empower
Those who would morally cower;
Betraying indifference
To their own existence;
Those who would lie
And deny,
Seek to dethrone
The One blissfully alone –
And rarely, if ever, truly atone?

The angels of the heavenly host –
Who long had revelled in the boast
That they alone had his attention –
Could not believe this intervention:
What prompted God to set his hand
To a covenant of being with creatures of land,
Whose main pursuit would be pleasure,
While rarely applying a spiritual measure?

'Allow me, Lord, to have my say' —
A cheery cherub from the Milky Way
Interrupted boldly in full flow
The One Above who best must know.

'What sort of plan
Is a son of man?' —
The cherub rather timidly began,
Quaking at his own lack of tact,
To question what was
Manifest fact.

But God frustrated his fulmination,
Expressing his own determination:

*'My will be done! Let there be light!*
*A measured time for day and night;*
*Let rain descend from skies above,*
*To quench the thirst of my man*
*And his love.*

*'Let oceans of water the earth embrace,*
*Let rivers and streams zigzag the space*
*That I'll create for the human race.*

*'Let sun and moon and earth rotate,*
*So human life may generate,*
*Where cool and cold and warmth and heat*
*Entice my nature to yield her treat.*

*'Let there be hills, and dales below,*
*And fields so green where man might sow*
*The seeds for fruit and roots to grow;*
*Where cows and geese and lambs and cats,*
*Nifty mice and lively rats,*
*Gaze with envy at the bats*
*And their flying friends who stop for chats*
*Out of reach of their land-based cronies,*
*Like the lofty giraffes and children's ponies.'*

'But, Lord,' a senior Seraph called,
Hitherto by God's word enthralled:
'May I, your humble servant, say
A word in your ear about the way
Your universe will no longer be
Subject to your royal decree.

'For rumour has it in the heavenly portals,
That you wish to share with mere mortals
The power, the knowledge and the glory,
For them to create their own story;
Imperiously strutting the stage of life,
Making a virtue of war and strife.

'For they will plunder and they will kill,
Their voice will thunder and not be still,
Demanding of others
To do their will.

'Chariots of war they'll design,
Missiles with targets they'll align,
Women and children
Who've committed no crime,
Will suffer the most
Every time.

'The earth will be filled with the blood of the just,
Remorseless victims of violence and lust,
Of power-crazed monsters with hearts of lead,
Who spare no thought for how many fall dead.
For the anguish of parents they'll not care,
Mourning sons who lie
They know not where.

'So,' said that Seraph,
'Is that what you'd bless:
A world of darkness,
Mankind in distress?
Will you in the future
Have no such regret?
Will you never view
Your man as a threat?'

*'Silence, Seraph! Speak not of regret;*
*Seek not to change my higher mind-set.*
*"Regret" is a term of man's invention,*
*Fearing the folly of his former intention.*

*'But I, by time, am not constrained,*
*The past by me can be reframed;*
*It is never gone from my sight,*
*It cannot darken what I coloured bright.*
*The future's not a thought unborn,*
*A sun awaiting a new day's dawn.*
*I am the present, I am the past;*
*I'm from the first until the last,*
*I will,*
*I act,*
*I embrace;*
*All that exists —*
*I am its place.*

*'Whatever your view of humankind,*
*I will never change my mind.*
*I know his violence and his greed,*
*But within his heart I'll plant the seed*
*Of righteousness and of the need*
*To seek me out and make of earth*
*A paradise of infinite worth,*
*Where love and peace and truth abound,*
*And stilled forever will be strife's sound.'*

# *Adam*
## (2:7–20)

So Adam appeared at the divine behest,
All innocence, and walking undressed;
Head held high,
In his step a spring,
Overwhelmed with wonder
At everything
That caught his eye as he stepped into life –
As yet alone,
Without a wife.

Pure goodness,
Bathed in primordial light;
Energy of a meteorite;
But one whose seed –
Through lust or greed,
A parent's over-expectation,
A sibling's dare, a friend's temptation,
A colleague's envied reputation,
A thoughtless word or prevarication –
Would be deaf to his Maker's exhortation.

'*I've called you Adam,*
*I like that name;*
*Conflicting concepts*
*It seeks to proclaim:*
*From* adamah — *the earth below,*
*Or from* demut, *divinity's glow.*

'*If you are anchored in physicality,*
*And have no truck with spirituality,*
*Then you're* adamah *in reality,*
*And your life will be a vague vacuity.*

'*But if your sights are set on high,*
*And you have faith when others deny;*
*If your deeds are good and true,*
*And acts of kindness you accrue,*
*Then my* demut *you'll share with pride —*
*And you'll always find me by your side.*'

'Oh, heaven-bound I'll surely be,'
Said Adam with alacrity.
'*Of course you will,*' was God's reply —
Without conviction, and with a sigh!

'*Of course you will; you'll pray and sing,*
*Read my Scriptures and make bells ring;*
*You'll initiate those newly born —*
*And massacre those who don't conform!*

'*Be not perplexed, my little man,*
*For that is not my ideal plan;*
*But I grant freedom to your kith and kin,*
*To opt for good or to sin.*
*For they're not puppets on a string,*
*Nor celestial angels on the wing;*
*They're men and women I've designed,*
*With a complex, independent mind.*

*'With justice they'll acquit or harm,*
*To wounds apply a soothing balm;*
*The harassed in spirit they will calm,*
*And the gullible they'll cheerfully charm!*
*But they will also cause alarm*
*When they threateningly raise a muscled arm,*
*And strike the weak without a qualm,*
*Pillaging the victor's palm.'*

'So what's the point, Lord, of my life,
If wickedness is so rife;
If attaining good is such a struggle,
As ephemeral as a bubble?

'And where will you be when the weak
In fear cry out – or fear to speak;
When mothers cradle to their breast
The erstwhile glory of their nest:
Lifeless victims of a violent quest
By men to re-order, at their own behest,
A fractured world,
As they think best?'

*'Enough of your questions, Adam, my friend,*
*Now let your ear to me attend:*
*Through adamah's prism you're viewing man's fate,*
*But I, at the end of time, await*
*A mankind exhausted from its dark deeds,*
*A coming together of disparate creeds,*
*A true empowerment of the weak,*
*A banishment of the evil streak.'*

'But just how long, Lord, will all that take,
For a human-kind with so much at stake?'

'Although I've said enough of "why?"
I'll offer you this, my last reply:
There've been other worlds before this one,
Which I've dispatched to oblivion,
When man left me no other choice,
Having suppressed his moral voice;
When nations passed beyond redemption,
With kindness meriting no mention.
Those worlds then vanished without a trace —
And with them went their human race.

'But a time will come — I have no doubt —
When a world will be born to take up the shout:
"Praise the Lord from the heights!"
When a new Adam will raise his sights
Heavenward,
And, pure of heart,
Seek its guidance from the start;
And without so much as a trace of guile,
Be filled with love and a ready smile,
For fellow man in far off isle,
Whom he will greet with "Shalom, brother!"
And never think of as just "another;"
Moulding all his generations
Into a family of bonded nations,
Attentive to all of my orations.'

'Will *mine* be that world, Lord?
Will *it* seek to promote accord?
Will *my* offspring earn your grace,
And eternally behold your face?'

Adam stood waiting for a reply,
Till the sun went down in the sky;
Desperate to hear of his children's fate,
He scanned the heavens to locate
The One who, mysteriously,
Was making him wait.

'Why, Lord, this long delay?' –
He bellowed loudly till the break of day,
His face awash with his tears –
But with no response to allay his fears.

'I will not move from my place,
Till you tell me the future of my human race,'
Cried Adam weakly as he fell to the ground,
Closed his eyes, and, without a sound,
Slipped into an induced sleep –
And dreamt of deer, gazelles and sheep.

# Eve
## (2:21–25)

He felt a pressure on his thigh,
And sensed the presence of God close by;
A sudden surge of strange elation,
Followed by a vague sensation,
Of being opened up and then sewn –
Before waking up,
No more alone.

Before him stood a vision unique,
Beauty encased in a slight physique;
Lustrous hair, rounded hips,
Star-like eyes and full red lips.

His gaze she met with a smile of joy,
Coy and demure – that feminine ploy –
Was how she chose to be revealed
To the one with whom her fate was sealed.

'*You,*' said God,
'*Are the first man of all;*
*I'll bless and preserve you,*
*And let you walk tall.*
*Eve is the one you'll love and hold,*
*She'll raise your spirits and warm you when cold;*
*She'll add to the beauty of all I've created,*
*And bear your children*
*When you both have mated.*

'*Call her Eve, meaning "mother of life,"*
*For she is your partner as well as your wife;*
*She'll share all your joys, as well as your pain —*
*And clip your feathers when you get too vain!*

'*She'll make of your house*
*A home to enjoy,*
*And bless you in time*
*With a girl or a boy;*
*She'll open her door to those in need,*
*And help even before they plead.*
*She'll let you think that you are master,*
*And she fragile as alabaster;*
*But in truth she's made from bone so tough,*
*That she can cope with smooth and rough;*
*And though she may neither hunt nor build —*
*But knead the flour that she's milled,*
*And feed her family the choicest fare,*
*And offer to it her love and care —*
*She's a lioness in her lair,*
*And the ill-disposed should best beware,*
*And camouflage their hostile stare,*
*And think again if they appear*
*To threaten those that she holds dear.*
*And though her mate may despair,*
*She remains well aware,*
*That chances oft are offered late,*
*To restore man's fortune and estate.*

'So listen well to her advice,
For if you don't, you'll pay a price;
And regard her caution as a chance,
To attain your goal and to advance.'

# Garden of Eden
## (2:8–17)

To Adam and Eve came the Lord's word:
'To you both it may sound absurd,
But you must work to earn your keep,
And only when you sow
You'll reap.

'This Garden, called Eden, in which you stand,
Is not the only piece of land
Where I could have housed the human race,
But I preferred to choose this place,
For it to thrive and have its space;
Because it is uniquely lush,
And every tree and plant and bush,
Is specially crafted by my hand,
As is every grain of sand,
Washed by rivers undulated,
Tossing treasures unabated.

'River Pishon flows with gold,
Pearls and onyx, wealth untold,
River Gihon circles Cush,
Yielding little but bulrush;
The Tigris and Euphrates long,
Embrace Ashur like a thong;
Its banks a home to swamp and lake,
Migrating bird and poisonous snake.

A vast store of living treasure,
Have I created for your pleasure.
Look around you for a while,
See, there lies a crocodile,
Chewing on a rattlesnake,
Without a sign that he's awake.
'But when the unwary display no fear,
He suddenly strikes from front or rear;
In the blinking of an eye,
He will pounce on those nearby.

'My Garden is home to countless beast,
Bulls and cows and calves and geese,
Billy goats and buffalo,
And ibex that won't say, 'hello!'
Sheep and pigs, and dogs that bark,
Owls that see well in the dark;
Stag and hart and buck and doe –
Some are friends, and others foe.

'Birds that soar so high in the sky,
And those that prefer to glide close by;
Blackbird, vulture, dove and thrush,
Alighting briefly on tree and bush.

'Eagle, kestrel, falcon, hawk;
Some that sing, and some that squawk.
Hear the parrot when he tries to talk,
Watch peacocks strut while others walk;
Songbirds, warblers, lapwing and rook,
That pity you, Adam, when they take a look
At you dawdling, eyes to the ground,
Missing so much of nature's sound,
Yet wishing you too could be heaven-bound.

'We've now arrived at Eden's centre,
A gated Garden that you may enter;
Look around in each direction,
Fields and fruit ripe to perfection.

'Turf and grass and papyrus,
Luscious umbelliferous,
Boughs and plants of every hue,
Bathing in the morning dew.

'Lofty trees, so tall, so proud,
Bidding "good day!" to the passing cloud;
Showing their age through nature's etching,
Branches, like man's arms, outstretching,
Inviting the artist, skilled at sketching;
Birds, their nesting foliage fetching.

'Acacia, elm, palm and cedar,
Olive, plane and box;
Fruit trees to be enjoyed,
And hedge to make woodblocks.

'Every tree and plant and seed,
Fruit and green and herb and weed,
I've created for your need —
With just one rule to which you'll accede:

'The trees of knowledge and of life,
Are not for you or for your wife;
Their properties are not for mortals,
But for those who inhabit heavenly portals.

'Now you've dominion over all I've made,
Attend to none who would dissuade
You in any single, minute matter –
By bribe, threat or deceptive chatter –
From keeping my charge to the letter.
Custodians be,
That none may better.

'Know that I look down at you,
At all times for any clue
That you're remiss in any way.
Beware, my children,
If you stray!'

# Lilith and the Serpent
## (Folklore)

The temptress, Lilith, a spirit of the night,
Was desperate to put Eve to flight,
So that, with Adam, she might unite,
And he be banished from the Lord's sight;
That his brave new world might be aborted,
And his Maker's dream once more
Be thwarted.

'Eve, my beauty,' she cooed with a smile,
To cover her incorrigible guile,
'Let me advise you on affairs of the heart,
Because, therein, I'm incomparably smart.

'The first rule a woman must know,
Is a man needs time and space to grow,
To think and plan, to dream and pray –
If he is not to walk away.

'He'll miss you more when you're not there,
And never doubt your love and care;
He'll respect you knowing you've explored
The entire Garden –
And be assured,
That your advice
Won't go ignored.'

So Eve set off to see the sights,
And to sample the delights
Of the Garden that was now her home,
Where she and Adam were free to roam,
Either together or alone.

But no sooner had she left
When Lilith – in the occult deft –
Fashioned herself into another Eve,
With the intention to deceive
Adam –
And with him to cleave!

Lustrous hair, rounded hips,
Star-like eyes and full red lips –
Every subtle intonation,
Every cute gesticulation,
Even to the imprint of Eve's feet,
With the heel appearing
Incomplete.

'Adam, my new husband,
The time has surely come
For you to show your love for me
Before the day is done.
The good Lord has made me
From the hard bone of your thigh,
But when I look into your eyes,
I melt into a sigh.

'Hold me in your arms so strong,
And put your lips to mine,
For this you'll find more pleasurable
Than the choicest wine.'

Adam enclosed her in his arms,
And put his lips to hers;
Surrendering to her charms,
Delighting in her purrs.

Just then there came a mighty flash
Of lightning so bright,
That struck Lilith on her face
And sealed her lips quite tight.

'*Lilith,*' thundered the divine voice,
 '*You have no part to play*
*In Adam's fall from heavenly grace* –
*Let Eve lead him astray!*'

## *Eating of the forbidden fruit*
### (3:1–24)

On Eve's return from her lengthy tour
She passed the forbidden trees;
By contrast all the rest seemed poor –
By desire she was strongly seized.

A hidden force propelled her
To approach as close as she might;
She struggled to avert her eyes
To shut out the rapturous sight.

But Lilith's wiles, ever strong,
Diverted Eve from right to wrong;
To further her original plan,
With guile to seize Eve's gullible man.

A serpent, born of Lilith's occult power,
Lurked in the shadow of a fragrant bower,
Close by where Eve stood, quite mute,
Overcome with desire to eat the fruit.

'Eve,' spoke the serpent, in a voice so soft,
Holding the forbidden fruit aloft,
'Is this not the object of your heart's desire?
Now, have *I* incurred the good Lord's ire?'

'But he commanded *us*,
Not you,' said Eve,
'Those two trees alone to leave,
Without so much as the slightest touch,
Or even the very barest brush
Against its trunk or branch or root –
Let alone to eat its fruit!
And if his word we defy,
The sentence is that we must die.'

'Oh, Eve,' said the serpent, 'you foolish child,
How little you fathom the Lord's mind;
He was simply giving you a test,
To see how determined you were to wrest
The choicest blessing from his treasure chest.

'For one of the trees whose fruit you desired
Will impart knowledge that, once acquired,
Will make you as wise as the Lord –
And that, be sure, he can ill afford
If he wishes to remain alone adored.'

With that, the wily serpent unfurled
His slithery body and suddenly hurled
Eve roughly against that choice tree,
Gashing her shoulder and grazing her knee,

'See you've touched the taboo tree,'
Said the serpent, exuding glee,
'And if he warned you that you'd die,
Now you see it was a lie.
So if in touching all was well,
To desist from eating he can't compel.'

'Thank you, serpent, for your wise advice.'
She tasted the fruit – 'That was really nice!'
Rushing to Adam, she bestowed a kiss,
And, beholding his sheer bliss,
When his lips opened wide –
A slice of the fruit Eve slipped inside.

No sooner had Adam ceased to chew,
When a foreboding they both never knew
Gripped them as they became aware
That their God was also standing there.

Glancing guiltily at each other,
They sensed a powerful need to cover
Parts of their bodies hitherto shown,
Whose shame for them had not been known.

'Oh, Adam,' boomed God, '*you foolish sinner!*
*You could have been an eternal winner!*
*Why have you so betrayed my trust?*
*Why did you not control your lust?*'

'It wasn't me, Lord' Adam whimpered,
'I would never have been so blinkered
As to think of disobeying your will,
Just for the sake of a passing thrill.

'It's the woman you gave me who's to blame –
She's the one devoid of shame.
She deceived me into eating;
She desired the pleasures fleeting.'

*'Eve,' said God, 'that's Adam's defence.*
*Should I now proceed to pass sentence?*
*Did you not, indeed, exploit his lust? –*
*Defend yourself if you must!'*

'God, I beg you, don't judge me in haste.
Indeed, I enjoyed the fruit's taste;
But I was a victim of the serpent's ruse,
When he colluded with Lilith to seduce.'

*'I hear you,' said God. 'The serpent I'll question.*
*No doubt he'll have a cogent suggestion*
*As to whom I should punish, Adam or Eve,*
*And why him alone I should mercifully leave.*

*'One more thing – and I don't wish to be crude –*
*But since you're unhappy in the nude,*
*I've brought you fig leaves attached with laces,*
*To cover those mysterious places,*
*Whose display was never taboo,*
*But is now considered so by you.*

*'Among their tasks is to kindle the fire*
*Of what will be known as sexual desire,*
*Which, in turn, will lead to procreation,*
*And the birth of earth's founding nation.'*

God turned to the serpent: *'What have you done now?*
*Did I not insist that you take a vow*
*To live in peace with the man I'd made,*
*And do nothing at all to make him afraid?*

'Now, through you, Eve has sinned,
While you stood by and inanely grinned;
At your door I must lay the blame –
Your bond with man will never be the same.'

'Lord,' you know me better than that!
Would I behave like a boorish brat?
Eve was not misled by me;
It was but Lilith's trickery.

'She envied Eve the man she'd wed,
For Lilith desired to share his bed.
She created me to bring Eve down,
So she could don her bridal gown.'

'Enough!' cried the Lord, 'I've heard it all:
Because it's truly a very close call,
The blame shall be spread among all you three,
For eating the fruit of my precious tree.

'From this Garden Adam shall be sent
To a world where his strength will be spent
In sowing, planting, and harvesting grain,
In clearing, weeding, pruning – and pain,
As thorns and thistles tear at his skin,
As seasons pass when the yield is so thin
That he can barely feed the little mouths at his table –
Those he will name Seth, Cain and Abel.

'Eve, for diminishing your Adam's worth,
Your pain will be great when you give birth.
He'll be the one to give the commands,
And you will be putty in his hands.

'Serpent, I'll pull you down a peg,
To crawl on your belly, instead of your leg;
Man will forever be your foe,
He'll strike your head; you'll bite his toe.

*'I'll deal with you, Lilith, in my own good time,*
*Till then be confined to hot quicklime;*
*You're meant to tempt man as I require,*
*Not to satisfy your own desire.*

*'In case he attempts to return to the Garden,*
*I'll provide it with a cherubic warden,*
*Wielding a sword constantly turning –*
*Man's machinations wisely discerning.*

*'Too much freedom I've dispensed,*
*Now a new era has commenced,*
*When man shall be judged on account of his deeds,*
*And have to provide for his own needs.'*

# Cain & Abel
## (4:1–16)

Some time later Eve felt sick,
And noticed her stomach getting thick;
She couldn't do the household chores,
Or eat the food within her stores.

Adam feared that Eve would die,
And he thought he knew the reason why:
'This must be for having eaten the fruit.
God is clearly in hot pursuit!'

'*Adam,*' called God, in a gentle voice,
'*Don't be afraid, just rejoice;*
*For your wife, Eve, shall bear you a son,*
*Call him Cain and teach him to run,*
*To till the ground and hunt for his food –*
*Keeping him ever in a confident mood.'*

Cain was born before very long,
Followed by Abel, who wasn't too strong;
So Abel tended the goats and sheep –
And prayed each night before going to sleep.

Since, when they grew up, they'd need a wife,
God had blessed the mother of life;
For, when Adam and Eve together had lain,
Twin sisters were born with Abel and Cain.

Abel married his sister,
For which he offered thanks,
Through songs of praise and sacrifice
By the tranquil banks
Of the Pishon River
Where he gifted to his Lord
The fattest lambs of all his flocks –
Devotedly procured.

A fire came down from heaven
And swiftly devoured his lambs;
And Abel knew that the Lord
Had received them from his hands.

When Cain saw that his brother
Had received divine good will,
He thought, as firstborn, he'd receive
Something better still.

So he took a bath and combed his hair,
Selecting the best he had to wear;
But the fruit he chose was of inferior kind,
And, with little devotion in his mind,
He tossed it nonchalantly on the ground,
Not even shaping it into a mound.

The voice he heard from above
Was clearly of one quite riled:
*'Is that your token of love, Cain? –*
*From now you are exiled!'*

'But, Lord,' said Cain, self-righteously,
'Do you really think that's fair?
The entire earth is yours alone,
So why should you even care
Whether the gift I offer to you is
A harvest or one pear?'

*'Oh, stupid man,'* the Lord replied,
*'How could you fail to see*
*That it's the fruit of the heart that I desire,*
*Not what you offer me?*

*'But that is not your only sin,*
*From which your exile flows;*
*It's for what you did to your brother's wife,*
*The sister whom he chose.*

*'Not content with the wife you gained –*
*Whose love you don't deserve –*
*To seize Abel's, you felt constrained,*
*Thinking I didn't observe.*

*'A wife is sacred to her man –*
*That was built into my original plan.*
*I created them, body and soul,*
*To occupy the same bed roll.*

*'Because Abel's trust you violated,*
*Through the act you perpetrated,*
*His broken heart I must repair*
*Through blessings galore – but you beware,*
*One wanton glance at his wife,*
*And you will pay with your life!'*

Cain went away in disgrace,
But God's last words he couldn't efface;
They rang in his ears that were still burning
From God's warning and his own yearning.

'*Pay with your life!*' – Hmm! There's a thought.
Why should I remain so distraught?
With Abel gone, the reward will be great:
God's love for him will evaporate –
And I'll inherit his wife and his estate!'

One day the brothers were alone,
When Cain picked up the largest stone,
And smashed it over Abel's head –
And in an instant, he was dead!

'*Where's your brother?*' boomed the voice.
'I know not, Lord? Do I rejoice
In being his keeper wherever he goes?
You know he has so many foes.
Perhaps he was mauled by a lioness –
There are none who are quite so heartless
When they're protecting a young cub –
Or on the receiving end of a snub!'

'*Cain, I'll seal your lips together;*
*What a puerile attempt by you to weather*
*The storm of blame for a heinous crime –*
*I shall bury you in the fullness of time!*'

'Lord,' said Cain, 'please hear me out.
I know I've been a terrible lout,
But no one's ever been killed before,
Except for lion, a bear or boar.
How could I have guessed what now I know
That a man can die from a gentle blow?
So forgive me Lord before it's too late –
I acknowledge my sin and accept my fate.'

Thereupon, God replied,
*'I'll ignore the fact that you lied.*
*If in remorse you'll be resolute,*
*Your punishment I'll now commute.*

*'But the ground which absorbed Abel's blood*
*Will no longer yield its crop;*
*A fugitive and a wanderer be,*
*Scavenging food at very stop.'*

'But what,' said Cain, 'of the animals wild,
When they learn of this, my fate?
They'll regard me as an easy prey,
For them or for their mate.'

*'On that score, you need not fear,'*
God reassured Cain.
*'I've placed a sign between your eyes –*
*A reddish-coloured stain.*

*'The animals will know what that implies,*
*And keep you far from harm;*
*Seven-fold shall their punishment be*
*If they disturb your calm.*

*'Now off you go with your wife;*
*Search out the land of Nod.*
*Be fruitful there and multiply –*
*And submit yourself to God.'*

# Noah and the Ark
## (6:9–7:16)

Though God was filled with apprehension,
His forgiveness had no limitation;
So he waited without hesitation,
For clear portents of civilisation.

He even extended unto man,
Six or seven-fold his life's span,
That he might entreat the Lord's pardon,
In his desire to return to Eden's Garden.
But theft, murder and selfish design,
Gluttony, whoring and dependence on wine –
These were but some of man's many temptations –
Hardly the stuff with which to build nations!

Ten generations on, and the Lord still waited
In vain for man, of sin, to be sated;
But Cain's offspring were stony of heart –
Man and his maker were poles apart.

So God took the initiative,
And created a man called Noah;
A pious man, of simple tastes,
A boat-smith and a rower.

*'Alas, the world has failed the test,'*
Said God to him one day;
*'Apart from you, all the rest*
*In a flood I'll wash away.*

*'I'll start afresh with you and yours,*
*Giving freedom a second chance;*
*Though when I informed the heavenly host,*
*They just looked, disdainfully, askance.'*

'But God,' said Noah in reply,
'Do you truly wish that they should die?
What if they choose to repent,
And on remorse are wholly bent?'

*'Noah, do not lecture me,*
*I know what is just;*
*Ten generations I've tolerated*
*The worst of human lust.*

*'Idols of silver,*
*Of gold and stone,*
*Idols of copper*
*And animal bone,*
*They've erected in every place,*
*Petitioning fervently for their grace.*

*'Men lie with their neighbour's wife,*
*And if she cries out, she pays with her life;*
*No property is safe in its owner's domain –*
*The time has come to bring my rain!'*

'You know best,' said Noah,
'But why punish with rain?
Is that because drowning
Involves the most pain?'

*'No,'* said the Lord,
*'That was not in my mind.*
*I chose the rain*
*To save mankind.*
*'For you alone will have the means*
*To avoid the devastation;*
*You'll build an ark to my design,*
*To escape the inundation.*

'Of Gopher wood, stable and stout,
Sealed with pitch, in and out;
Three hundred cubits by fifty wide,
To ride the waves of the roughest tide.

'A window install in the topmost deck,
From where you'll view the pitiful wreck
Of homes that once were tall and grand –
The finest structures in the land –
Now flotsam tossed on heaving waves,
A floating mass of boards and staves,
In the seething swirl of the savage storm
That obliterates every form.

The middle storey allocate
To each animal and its mate,
So that when the waters do abate,
They can, once more, propagate.

The lowest storey is the store,
For food and water
And anything more
That you may bring to make your stay
More comfortable in any way.'

'Lord,' said Noah,
'How much time have I got? –
For this mammoth task,
I'll need a lot!'
'Will one hundred years suffice?'
Came God's reply, as cold as ice.

'Slowly, but surely,
The material hoard,
And then, without haste,
Cut every board.

'A model of the ark first create
For all to come and see,
For that, for sure, will excite
Their curiosity.

'"Noah," – expect them to ask –
"What is all this for?
Why invest in a ship so large
Given that you're so poor?
Do you intend to sail in it
Across uncharted sea,
To rediscover for yourself,
Adam's special tree?

'"Do you expect to succeed,
Where he miserably failed?
As its rightful owner
Do you expect to be hailed?"

'With patient conviction, you reply:
"It's to save me when you all die
By a terrible flood that will bring
Total destruction to everything.

'"Because man's sin has polluted the earth,
And of righteousness there's such a dearth,
Save my wife, sons and daughters-in-law –
With the rest of you all,
The Lord is at war.

'"So pray to him and acknowledge your sin;
Perhaps there's still time for you to win
A late reprieve from his decree –
And let's hear no more of Eden's tree!" '

Noah did as commanded,
The boards he cut and then he sanded,
Before attaching to an outline cast,
And sealing with pitch from base to mast.

During all those years people came to view,
And – to give Noah his due –
He bore their insults and their jibes,
Smiling warmly at them and their wives,
Assuring them of God's protection,
If they would only abandon
Their disaffection.

As the allotted time drew close to its end,
The animals were moved to wend
Their way toward Noah's ark,
By day and night, through light and dark,
Knowing instinctively the rendezvous,
They arrived in formation, two by two.

After one hundred and twenty years,
Exactly to the hour –
It began with a few gentle drops,
Then developed into a shower.

Then forty days of heavy rain,
Rendering sodden the entire terrain;
And the mockers of Noah's prognostication
Now became filled
With trepidation.

They heard a voice from heaven one day,
Calling Noah to make his way
With his family into the Ark –
As it grew unnaturally dark!

A mob then gathered and took up the cry,
'How can God leave us all to die?
'Let's burn the ark and thwart his plan,
So he'll have to save us with his favoured man.'

God sent some lions to forestall their attack
And protect the ark at front and back.
Not one further step could the mob now take
As the rainwater swelled to the size of a lake.

Noah and family made good their escape,
When the angel Gabriel wrapped them in his cape;
Raising them gently into the air,
And into the ark and the good Lord's care.

# Life in the Ark
## (whimsical)

Noah's surviving family
Had to sacrifice their rest;
Feeding all the animals
And cleaning up their mess.
Around the clock they laboured
Without an hour's sleep,
As each and every animal
Had its routine to keep.

The lions called for their food at dawn,
The giraffes dined at seven;
The tigers and the cockatoo,
Ate at eleven.
The partridge and the pheasant
Ate salad with the mousse,
At eight every morning
They were joined by the goose.

The goats and the lambs —
Used to snacking at noon —
Resented their place
Next to the baboon.

Early in the afternoon
The elephants would arrive,
Trumpeting their choice of food,
Vine branches dipped in chive.

The lazy crocodiles
Arrived there around three,
Expecting their favourite eating spot
Always to be free.

Twelve pails of water
Noah dragged in around four,
To be downed by the camels
Before they ate their straw.

Between the hours of five and six
The asses trotted by,
Savouring their barley soufflé
And sweet apple pie.

Seven in the evening,
When the sun had gone down,
The two bears would arrive,
Invariably with a frown;
For they greatly missed the hunt,
The chase and the kill,
And the juicy flesh of their victims —
Ah, they could taste it still!

Noah was an old man,
Six hundred years of age;
This mission was hastening
The on-set of dotage.

But God had kept his family alive,
Promising them they'd all thrive;
That the animals would have their allotted space,
In a world renewed
By heaven's grace.

## 'Testing the Waters'
(7:17–9:17)

Meanwhile, outside the ark
God's words all came true:
All manner of fish and animals
Perished in the brew.

One hundred and fifty days elapsed,
And the waters began to subside;
When the tops of the mountains came into view,
Noah's family cried.

A further forty days they sat
Inside the ark entombed,
Until Noah released a raven
When he thought dry land had loomed.

The raven flew back and forth,
But found no stick or grain
With which to build a cosy nest
And lay its eggs again.

Another seven days ensued,
And Noah dispatched a dove,
But finding no place for the sole of its foot,
It returned in a huff.

Seven days on, and Noah called,
'Out you go again!'
So the dove flew off, and behold! –
It found subsiding rain.

With a chirp and a whoop,
And a graceful swoop,
It plucked an olive leaf,
And took it back to the ark
To the family's great relief.

Seven days on, it was again dispatched,
And, discovering dry ground,
It liberated itself from the ark –
To the future wholly bound.

God called out to Noah,
One clear and sun-drenched morn,
*'You've kept my charge,*
*Preserving life,*
*As to the manner born.*

*'You and your wife I will bless*
*With everything you wish;*
*Shem, Ham and Japhet*
*Will multiply like fish.*
*When you dandle on your knees*
*Their newborn girls and boys,*
*None shall compare to you,*
*In the abundance of your joys.*

*'The longed-for day has now come*
*To bid farewell to the ark;*
*To the foot of Mount Ararat,*
*It will slowly drift and park.*

*'Now, when you see a rainbow,*
*Following the rain,*
*Let that be my special sign*
*That in future I'll refrain*
*From sending a fearful flood*
*To inundate the earth;*
*And I'll forgive man his shortcoming,*
*And recognise his worth.'*

# Noah's Last Days
## (9:18–27)

Noah lived the good life,
Planting many vine,
Doing lots of gardening
And downing his fine wine.

So drunk he became one day,
That he lay naked in his tent;
His grandson, Canaan, peeped in
And immediately sent
A message to his father, Ham,
Saying, 'Grandpa's got no shame,
So how can you describe him as
A man of great fame?'

Ham went to Noah's tent,
To check his son's account;
Seeing his father's nakedness,
He immediately ran out
And told his brothers that their dad
Deserved respect no more,
For, since the days of Adam and Eve,
Nakedness was against the law!

The brothers, Shem and Japhet
Deplored their father's plight;
They seized a large jacket
And, not gazing at the sight,
Covered up their sleeping dad,
Who, oblivious, just snored,
While they planted a kiss on his cheek –
His dignity restored.

In a dream, God told Noah
About Ham and Canaan his son,
And Noah solemnly announced
That their blessing would be undone.

'Ham shall ever remain
To his brothers a lowly slave,
And Canaan, throughout the world,
Shall be accounted a knave.

'What he did to his grandpa
A byword shall become
For those who take advantage –
On purpose or for fun –
Of those who cannot help themselves,
And, instead of helping, run.

## Tower of Babel
### (11:1–9)

Noah's offspring kept together,
Living in one place;
Just like him they loved to build
Wherever there was space.

The same language they all spoke –
It was a sacred tongue;
The one that God would one day use,
To teach right from wrong.

But when their families grew in size
And their flocks consumed the grass,
They fixed their sights on Shinar,
A land so rich and vast
That it could accommodate everyone –
And its pasturage would last.

A sage among them added
That, once in two thousand years,
The heavens come close to touching earth –
An aberration of the spheres.

'So, if we link the two by a tower,'
He excitedly exclaimed,
'We'll climb to heaven and assume the power
That God has hitherto claimed.

'Then we'll live immortal,
And gain a name unique,
As the ones who vanquished heaven,
Decoding its mystique.'

Noah's kindred, to a man,
Gave their rapt attention
To this most audacious plan
For the eternity of their nation.

They all set to –
Man, woman and child –
Preparing mortar from whatever grew wild;
Pouring it into a brick-shaped mould,
And baking it in ovens,
Exactly as told.

One day, God arrived to see
How it had progressed.
That was the defining moment
When he chose to arrest
The building of the tower
That stretched into the sky,
The moment when he'd make man
Eat his humble pie.

*'Let the language they've all spoken*
*Be useless like a pot that's broken.*
*Not a single word shall they recall –*
*Contributing to their downfall.*

*'From now they'll talk in tongues diverse:*
*Some in prose and some in verse;*
*A few in words of just two letters,*
*Others out-talking their betters.'*

So, if one builder called for a spade or trowel,
He was handed instead a cloth or towel;
And if one sought mortar to secure a brick,
He was handed a scraper or yard stick.

That swiftly led to scuffles and fights
And builders being knocked down from the heights,
Breaking their necks in all that melee –
With the project abandoned
Before sunset that day.

God scattered the rebels all over the globe;
Their babble of tongues, like a daedal robe,
Proclaiming their unity but an illusion,
With a friendly greeting
Snubbed as an intrusion..

— ❧❧ —

# *Abram discovers God*
## (Midrash)

Can the whole world be wrong,
With just one child right?
Can men all walk in darkness
And just one see the light?

That small lad was Abram,
Born to Terach in the city of Ur,
Terach made the idols
For both rich and poor.

From Nimrod, King of Chaldea,
To the local blacksmith's wife,
He supplied them all with the gods
That controlled their very life.

Gods of wood, adorned with braid,
Gods of silver, gold and jade;
Tall gods, small gods, fat and thin,
All with the power to absolve any sin.

Placed outside the door of every tent,
To every plea they gave assent;
No voice; no 'yes'; no 'no'; no 'don't' –
The petitioners acted as was their wont!

Abram helped his dad to fell the trees,
To chop the wood and shave the leaves,
To season the timber until the time
When it was truly in its prime,
And deftly with a file and plane,
Shape it into a man–like frame
Which the God, Bel, infused with breath,
Investing it with power over life and death.

Another of Terach's idols
Was Astarte, queen of heaven,
Consort of Baal,
She was worshipped in seven
Countries of the east
By young men and women
Desperate for the fertility
For which they'd vainly striven.

Abram watched a purchaser
Taking home his god:
'Does it deserve a worshipper
When it cannot even nod?
How can all these grown-ups
Commit to their god's will,
When they are no more than bits of trees
That grew on yonder hill?

'Surely the one who made the tree
Is deserving of the praise?
I must discover his identity
And learn of his ways.

'I've seen the laden clouds
Giving drink to the seeds;
I've heard the whispering wind
Cool them with its breeze;
I've watched as the sun
Coaxes them to growth,
Yielding the harvest
That feeds every mouth.

'Perhaps these are the gods
To whom we should pray:
The sun god, Mcrodach,
Who shines forth by day;
Or the moon god, Sin,
Who rules her subjects by night,
Surrounded by her myriad stars —
A most majestic sight!

'But gods who create? —
That they cannot be;
And those who want proof of that
Should just consider me:
The seed of the ground
May be sown by man,
But who made my ancestor,
The very first Adam?

'Who gave him the power of speech,
The creativity of mind?
Who placed his grasp beyond his reach,
To enrich mankind?

'It had to be an eternal One
Who created out of nought;
Revealing himself to my mind,
Desperate to be sought.'

To Terach's workshop
He repaired the next day;
And while his father was at prayer,
He smashed his gods of clay.

The biggest one, with arms upraised,
He did not so much as prod;
A prop in his grandiose scheme
To bring people to God.

When Terach returned to his home
And saw the devastation,
He summoned his son, Abram,
Demanding an explanation.

''Twas not me! Certainly not,
Who committed this terrible sin;
But that big, big, god, with the axe in his hand –
It had to have been him!'

'What do you take me for, my son,
A foolish son of Belial?
That god could never raise a hand
To receive a bowl of cereal!'

'Exactly, father, just my point,'
Cried Abram with conviction;
'So how can men believe in its power,
If it's bound by such restriction?

'Can you not see in front of your eyes
That Creation conforms to a plan,
Worked out in every detail,
By one much greater than man?

'He is the Maker of heaven and earth,
The father of all mankind;
He was present at Adam's birth.
He's the all-knowing mind.

'He is at one with eternity,
By his word all things occur;
Those who believe in idols,
Do undoubtedly err.

'So praise my God and worship him,
That you may see the light;
And let us together aid mankind
To abandon wrong for right.'

Terach bowed to the ground
Acknowledging all he'd heard,
Worshipping the God he had now found,
Awaiting his sacred word.

*'Terach, I will bless you*
*Through Abram, your son;*
*In reward for his faith in me,*
*A great nation shall he become.*
*Stretching from Aram*
*To Canaan's gentle shores,*
*And down to the Sea of Egypt –*
*All that shall be yours.*

*'A promised land, called Israel,*
*Your offspring shall possess,*
*After four hundred years of exile*
*And unremitting stress*
*They'll return to reclaim it*
*And worship me there by name,*
*Crowning kings by River Gihon –*
*Monarchs of great fame.*

*'Holy priests shall minister*
*In a temple I'll design,*
*Where they will offer sacrifice*
*And libations of wine.*

'But Abram, your special son,
He sensed from the start,
The nature of reality
That was closest to my heart:
Not the gifts of great expense,
But the kindness men dispense:
Sharing their bread, not with me,
But with my children who go hungry.'

## Abram and the Promised Land
(12: 1–9)

'A word to you, Abram, my son,
King Nimrod has heard what you've done;
He seeks your life for impugning his faith,
So make haste to Canaan
Where you'll be safe.

'Here, Abram, you cannot thrive,
However earnestly you may strive
To live a life of godliness,
Pursuing inner happiness.
For the men of Chaldea –
Like their gods –
Have no idea,
They are at odds
With notions of eternity,
With seeds of spirituality,
With discovering the path to me;
They would rather bend the knee
And worship –
A tree!

*'But in Canaan, there you'll grow;*
*The seed of Israel there you'll sow.*
*There we'll live, side by side,*
*While you teach my humankind*
*To worship me and to find*
*Their humanity,*
*Their soul,*
*Their mind.'*

So Abram took Sarai, his wife,
And his nephew, Lot;
To Canaan they journeyed to start a new life,
In that God-directed spot.

Abram called on the men of the town,
While Sarai dropped in on the women;
They were met with joy –
Not a single frown –
As they taught what God had bidden.

And those townsmen then went around,
Convincing countless others
Of the truth of the Lord whom they had found –
And their fathers, sisters and brothers.

Abram and Sarai's fame grew
Among all the folk of the east;
Their tents bore signs to be seen from afar,
Inviting everyone in to feast.

They were blessed by God in every way,
With sheep and goats and guests to stay,
Who brought them gifts to show respect
For one, they knew,
Was God's elect.

## Sarai in Peril
### (12:10–20)

Canaan boasts few rivers,
And is dependent on the rain;
When it fails to fall on time
There's famine and no grain.

But Egypt's great River Nile –
However unfair! –
Has water in abundance,
With plenty to spare;
For twice a year without fail
Its banks overflow,
Feeding irrigation
To every field's furrow.

One year in Canaan,
There was nothing to eat,
So Abram and Sarai left for Egypt,
To buy their stock of wheat.

'Why are you so pensive?'
Asked Sarai of Abram.
'It's because of your beauty, dear,
That I must devise a plan.

'For when the Egyptians notice
That you're the fairest of them all,
They'll seize you for their Pharaoh,
And stuff me with gall.

'Say you are my sister;
Don't say you are my wife,'
Pleaded Abram with Sarai,
In fear for his life.

'For Pharaoh won't touch a woman
With a husband in tow;
So first he removes him from the scene,
Before humbling her so.

'But if you say you're a virgin
And I a brother dear,
They'll not only save my life,
But let you keep me near.'

'But husband,' shouted Sarai,
'I will struggle and scream,
If they ever try to drag me
Into Pharaoh's harem.'

'Have faith, my beloved,
God will save you from that fate.
Has he not promised us a child
To crown our marital state?'

Now when they arrived in Egypt,
It happened as he'd said:
Pharaoh seized poor Sarai
And took her to his bed.

But as he attempted
To force her to his will,
A fearful pain gripped him,
And made him feel quite ill.

From every single bedroom
Of his great royal palace,
Came the shrieks of his sons –
Stricken in their phallus.

It didn't take Pharaoh long
To identify his sin:
That it was Abram and Sarai's God
Whose patience had worn thin.

He begged their forgiveness,
Before sending them on their way,
Laden with gifts of gold and grain,
To sweeten a bitter stay.

A special gift he added
As they were about to depart:
A maid called Hagar with a smile
That had touched Sarai's heart.

But our naive matriarch
Was blissfully unaware,
That Hagar had been planted,
To serve as a snare,
By a devious Pharaoh
Who had hardened his heart,
And was determined to show Sarai
That she wasn't quite so smart!

## *Abram and Lot*
### (13:1–17)

Now the flocks of Abram's nephew, Lot,
Increased each passing week,
But when Abram asked him to account,
He just smiled and turned his cheek.

But it was clear as the noonday sky
That Lot's were ill-gotten gains,
That he'd instinctively steal and lie –
And wouldn't change his ways.

But he was not the main culprit;
There were also Lot's shepherds,
Who couldn't be dissuaded –
Despite Abram's best efforts –
From leading their flocks into others' fields,
Trampling their furrows
And devouring their yields.

'No longer let there be strife,
Between you and me,'
Said Abram to his nephew,
As they sat beneath a tree,
Seeking to resolve the matter
Coolly, one day,
While their flocks, disinterestedly,
Reclined, munching hay.

'The whole of our land is before us,
Choose wherever suits you best;
So that we may go our separate ways –
And I'll take the rest.'

So Lot chose the Jordan plain,
Well-watered from the river,
And pitched his tent with the men of Sodom –
Every man a sinner!

So uncle Abram took as his own
Canaan's western part –
More rugged, less productive –
To make his new start.

But God reassured him,
A great future was in store,
For this was the land of promise
For his offspring,
Evermore.

*'They will become as numerous*
*As the grains of the sand;*
*Though not by my blessing alone*
*Will they secure this land.*

*'Righteousness and sacrifice,*
*A book and a sword —*
*They are the prerequisites*
*For its award.*

*'So teach your children my statutes,*
*My laws and my ways,*
*That they may be deserving*
*Of my land and of my praise.'*

# Wars of the Kings
(14:1–24)

Abram used all Pharaoh's gifts
To recruit three hundred men,
Trained by Eliezer, his right-hand man,
On mountain, hill and fen.

A confederacy of four states,
Under Amraphel, the Babylonian king,
Waged war against Sodom
And the four chieftains under his wing.

Amraphel drove the Sodomites
Towards the valley of slime,
Where they sank into the soggy pits,
Out of which they couldn't climb.

The victors took all the spoils
Of the hapless King of Sodom,
And imposed forced labour upon Lot,
Nephew of Abram.

When Abram heard what had occurred,
He was roused to immediate action,
He marshalled his men
And put to flight
Amraphel and his faction.

To the king of Sodom he promptly restored
His crown and the booty seized;
Refusing spoil for himself,
Though the king appeared displeased.

When pressed to explain himself,
He readily replied:
'So that your majesty can never claim
That it was on you that I relied.

'The Almighty God whom I serve,
Will determine my just reward;
One blessed by his generous hand,
Not seized by the sword.'

# Sarai and Hagar
## (16:1–16)

Sarai's heart could not rejoice,
Nor was there laughter in her voice;
For decades had passed and she knew that soon
Time would deny her
The fruit of her womb.

'Husband dear,' she said one day,
'I've decided on some way
To gain fulfilment in my old age,
As well as to quell my inner rage
That motherhood will not be mine –
Take Hagar, my maid, as a concubine;
And the child she bears I'll embrace
As if it were my own,
By God's good grace.'

Sarai brought her to Abram's tent,
And Hagar conceived;
But she mocked her mistress's barren state –
And poor Sarai grieved.

'A friend of God, Sarai claims to be,'
Exclaimed Hagar contemptuously.
'For years with Abram she went to sleep,
Yet no reward did she ever reap;
Yet the night he took me as a mate,
I was blessed by God to procreate!'

Sarai was smitten with much self-doubt
When she heard that painful boast:
'I couldn't have lived a purer life –
I swear by the heavenly host!'

Beside herself, in deep despair,
Her stomach filled with bile,
She lashed out wildly at her maid –
Feeling all the more vile.

Hagar fell to the ground,
And clutched her swollen belly;
As Sarai watched her writhing in pain,
Her feet turned to jelly.

Hagar fled in terror
From her mistress's home,
In the direction of the desert,
In search of her own;
Desperate for the protection
Of her kith and kin –
High-born Egyptians,
From the town of Qasr Ibrim.

But the sun beat down and her water was spent,
A sand storm felled her make-shift tent;
Hagar wandered, the entire day,
Bitter in spirit –
The wrong way.

She collapsed by a well on the road to Shur,
Then heard a voice she could not ignore.
About to give in to total despair,
It greeted her gently,
Caressing the air:

'Hagar, my dear daughter,
What has brought you to your knees?
And why are your eyes red raw
With shedding salty tears?
'What are you doing alone in this place?
Forfeiting your mistress's grace?'

Hagar related
How she'd been abused;
But the angel retorted,
'I'm rather bemused
And disinclined to hear
Just one view,
When the guilt's finely balanced –
And, what about you?

'Did you not commit the very first offence,
Hurting Sarai's feelings and making her tense?
Demeaning yourself as consort of that sage –
So why be surprised at your mistress's rage?

'There's no escape for you just yet;
Return and bear their child.
Give him the name Ishmael,
And leave him to run wild.

'For he shall be an outlaw,
Hunting man and beast;
Embroiled in every skirmish,
And feared throughout the east.

'But God will avenge your suffering
At the hands of Sarai,
When the offspring of Ishmael
Make her descendants cry,
As each lays claim to a heavenly grace
Which the other, by force, shall deny.'

So Hagar returned to her mistress's home,
And in time gave birth to a child
Whom Abram loved and couldn't see
Was truly growing up wild.

# Circumcision and a change of name
## (17:1–27)

Abram was now ninety nine years;
Gripped by excitement when God appears
To him in a dream to confirm at first hand
His plan to give him the promised land:

'*You and Sarai shall have a son*
*In addition to Ishmael;*
*And the nations that proceed from them*
*Shall both revere your name.*

*Both branches will invoke you*
*As the founder of their clan;*
*Hence your name shall now be changed*
*To Abraham*
*From Abram.*

'*Abram – "exalted father" –*
*Is a family domain;*
*But Abraham extends its scope*
*To universal acclaim,*
*As "a father of many nations,"*
*All descended from Shem.*

'*Sarai means "my princess,"*
*A token of one man's love;*
*Let her now be called Sarah –*
*"Princess of the One Above."*

*Just as I protected you*
*From the designs of the Egyptian king –*
*By punishing him, pointedly,*
*In that self-same sinning limb –*
*So, as a sign forever*
*Of my love that shall not fail,*
*Shall your offspring circumcise,*
*At eight days,*
*Each new-born male.'*

## Visit of the Three Angels
### (18:1–22)

Abraham circumcised himself –
Without a moment's delay.
As did Ishmael and all the slaves –
Of faith, a grand display!

On the third day, feeling sore
And resting outside his tent,
Abraham noticed three wayfarers
Whose strength was almost spent.

He ran to meet them:
'My lords, come take a break,
Wash your feet and freshen up,
And eat some bread and cake.

He escorted them back to his home,
Summoning Sarah to help him prepare
Cakes and cheese, and the most tender meat –
Well done, medium and rare.

But Abraham didn't know
That they were angels sent by God.
'Where is Sarah?' one of them asked –
Which Abraham thought quite odd!

'She's in her tent,' he replied,
'Like any modest wife.'
'Well, tell her that within her womb
There stirs another life.'

But Sarah was now beyond her prime,
She'd enjoyed her best years;
She'd long since passed her monthly times,
Over which she'd shed her tears.

So when she heard those tidings,
As she stood behind the door,
She laughed at their import –
And got on with sweeping the floor!

But the angel was clearly not amused,
And told Abraham so:
'In nine months time – just mark my words –
You'll have a babe in tow!'

The second angel had a task,
To cure Abraham's pain,
'I've brought with me some special cream,
To heal your sore membrane.'

Abraham was about to offer thanks
When the third angel interposed:
'Sodom and Gomorrah's tragic fate
To you will be disclosed'

—— ✣ ——

# Sodom and Gomorrah

(18:23–33)

Sodom and Gomorrah had now sunk
To the nadir of wickedness;
Civilised living had given place
To total lawlessness.

Conscience was a weakness
They wouldn't tolerate;
Kindness displayed brought
Confiscation of estate.

Gangs of thugs roamed around,
Assailing all they met;
Beating people to the ground,
To steal what they could get.

Women's virtue was no more
Something to be prized;
Young and old alike were prey –
Morality was excised.

Daggers affixed to every belt,
Were drawn without hesitation;
And plunged into a stranger's heart
At the slightest provocation.

*'Their wickedness having gone*
*Far beyond the limit,*
*I'll raze those cities,'* thundered God,
*'That none might ever visit.'*

Abraham was so appalled
When he heard that decree;
That to his God he immediately called,
In spiritual agony.

'How can the judge of the whole earth
Act in such a way,
As to make those of true worth
With the wicked
Pass away?

'What if there are fifty men,
Good, kind and true,
Would you sweep them away in your wrath? –
Is that what you'd do?'

*'I hear you, Abraham, my friend,*
*I'll listen to your plea.*
*If I find fifty worthy men,*
*I'll grant them clemency.'*

'But God,' retorted Abraham,
'What about forty-five?
Do not so many righteous men
Deserve to survive?'

*'Of course they do;*
*I must concur,'*
Said God, indulgently.
'Then you'll also save forty!'
Said Abraham with alacrity.

'My God,' said he without a pause,
'Forgive my abundant cheek;
I have no right to intervene –
A mere human and so weak.
But if there are only thirty men
After your own heart,
Would you destroy those cities
And no mercy impart?'

*'You drive a hard bargain!'*

Said God in reply,
*'I can't ignore your earnest plea,*
*However hard I try.'*

'Then, Lord, since I've already become
An effective intercessor,
Would not twenty men also deserve
A fate that much better?'

*'Abraham, your response —*
*I really can't pretend —*
*Is much as I expected,*
*From my own cherished friend.'*

'God, I shouldn't do this,
But allow me one last plea:
Would not ten truly righteous men
Deserve an amnesty?'

*'Yes,' said God, 'for such men*
*The cities might have been saved;*
*But, sadly, I must warn you,*
*The result for which you craved*
*Will simply not materialise,*
*For they've all misbehaved.*
*Not one is worthy of your concern —*
*Go home, they're all unsaved!'*

## Lot and the destruction of the cities
### (19:1–29)

Two of the angels
Made straight for the city of Sodom,
Where Lot, ignoring protocol,
Invited them to his home.

After a meal they turned in for the night,
But heard a commotion outside;
The men of the place had surrounded the house,
And, to a man, they cried:
'Surrender unto us the guests you have,
So we may have our way with them,'
Lot went outside, locking the door,
To forestall any mayhem.

'Listen, my friends, to my voice:
To those men I gave my word;
By inviting them in,
I have no choice
But to defend them by the sword.

'Can't we, however, do a deal
To satisfy all our needs?
Take my virgin daughters,
But spare my guests, please.'

'How dare this foreigner bargain?'
Cried the mob as one.
'He deserves to be bound with a truss
In a very dark dungeon.
But not before we've taken our turn
To have some real good fun!'

Just as they surged forward
To seize the hapless Lot,
The angels emerged and raised their arms,
To foil their dastardly plot.

They smote the angry, seething crowd.
To a man they were struck blind;
Fleeing in every direction
And going out of their mind.

'Lot,' cried the angels,
'You need to get out of here!
Gather your wife and daughters,
But tell them not to fear;
For God is about to destroy
This entire place,
Anything that's left behind
Will disappear without trace.

'Consider yourselves fortunate
That you are to escape,
And that your two daughters
Were spared a terrible rape.
For none of you merit
To put God's mercy to the test –
For, if not for your uncle Abraham,
You'd have perished with the rest.

'Now, let's make haste along the road,
To Zoar we are bound;
But as the two cities explode
And you hear a frightful sound,
Do not be tempted, even once,
To look back to view their fate –
Let's be on our way speedily,
For the hour's already late.'

As God's fury unleashed on Sodom
And Gomorrah brimstone and fire,
Lot's wife turned round for one brief glance
At the red hot funeral pyre.

The searing sight of hell on earth,
Rooted her to the spot;
Her heart gave out as she screamed for help
From her husband, Lot.

Her body became encrusted
With the salt that blew around,
And she was preserved for a thousand years
As a pillar —
Well renowned.

## Lot and his daughters
### (19:30–38)

Lot and his daughters fled in fear
To a cave in a mountainside,
Where they stayed for many a year,
Losing all sense of pride.

One daughter said to the other,
'The Zoarites must also be dead,
So where will we find two suitors
To whom we might be wed?
But if God has destroyed his entire world,
Yet preserved us alive,
Then surely our task is to procreate
To enable it to survive.

'As I see it, there's but one male
To provide us both with seed,
And that is dad —
And I know it's bad —
But this *is* a critical need.

'Let's ply him now with plenty of wine,
The strongest he's ever produced,
And when he's drunk let's lie with him,
And let him be seduced.'

The girls lay down on succeeding nights
In their drunken father's bed,
Where they both conceived
And Lot became
To his own daughters wed!

The older girl, quite brazenly,
Called her son *Moab* – "From dad."
The younger named hers *Ben-Ami*,
"Of my people" –
A fine young lad.

# *Isaac and Ishmael*
## (21:1–21)

True to God's promise, Sarah gave birth
To a son called Isaac, meaning "laughter" or "mirth,"
Recalling the faith that she'd previously lacked,
That God renews bodies by old age once racked.
She'd laughed at that time at elderly passion;
Now her friends would laugh at her baby's milk ration!

But the child grew up in his father's tradition,
Believing in God and in his own mission:
To transmit the truth far and wide,
And be heaven's witness,
Through love and pride.

But Ishmael, his big brother,
Taunted him till he cried;
And his total lack of any faith
Was a thorn in Isaac's side.

'You worship a god,' mocked Ishmael,
'Whom you cannot see;
Claiming him as Creator –
What supreme folly!
You also waste all your time,
Doing righteous deeds,
And preaching to all and sundry
Against idolatrous creeds,
When you could be fishing and hunting wild deer,
Or quenching your thirst on wine and beer;
Lying in wait, to rob and maim,
Playing with friends a favourite game;
Admiring a maid in her skirt and blouse,
And seizing her as she milks the cows!'

Sarah overheard Ishmael's godless taunts,
And knew the whereabouts of his unholy haunts.
She feared the evil influence that he exerted,
And the cause of justice that he blithely perverted.

'We must drive him out,' she announced one day.
'I know in my heart that there's no other way
For us to preserve our home-life intact,
And never renege on the good Lord's pact.'

'We cannot do that,'
Was Abraham's reply.
'Surely he remains our son
Until the day we die!'

But God whispered in his ear
That he mustn't shed a single tear,
But banish Ishmael from his home
And leave him entirely free to roam
And do whatever he may please –
Leaving Isaac alone
And at ease.

So Hagar was banished with her son;
In Beer Sheba desert they strayed.
In time her reserves of water were gone,
So she raised her voice and prayed
To the God of Sarah and Abraham,
To have mercy on their handmaid.

As the sun beat down on Ishmael's head,
He collapsed –
And Hagar, filled with dread,
Dragged him to the shelter of a nearby shrub,
Squeezing out for him a ripe carob.

Then she heard a heavenly voice,
Giving her reason to rejoice:
A promise that Ishmael would soon proceed
To a destiny God had decreed.

'*Arise, seize hold of the lad's hand;*
*Look around and you shall see*
*Confirmation of my promise*
*That a great nation he shall be.*'

Hagar raised her eyes and saw
A well that had sprung into view;

She filled up the empty flasks
For herself and Ishmael too.

The lad revived and made his home
In that rugged, desert place,
Where, together with his many friends,
He'd hunt and roam and race.

In tests of strength he was the best –
Acclaimed a cut above the rest;
Acquiring much ill-gotten gain,
Head of a horde,
Inflicting pain;
Seizing other people's wives,
Begetting children,
Destroying lives.

# *Binding of Isaac*
(22:1–19)

Abraham walked in the light of his God,
Ever negating himself;
Valuing the spiritual,
Discounting material wealth.

Evolving into an ideal man,
Of whom future folk would say:
'He sensed what God required of him,
And responded without delay.'

Now, though God knew the strength of his faith,
And required no practical test,
Mankind was entitled to observe his resolve,
To become spiritually impressed.

So God was constrained to impose on his friend,
A trial that few could endure;
One that, beyond a shadow of doubt,
Would prove that his faith was pure.

'*Take your son, that Sarah has born,*
*The one that you both love more,*
*And offer him up at Moriah,*
*On a mount that you'll explore.*'

Abraham rose early next day,
While Sarah was still asleep;
He didn't tell her of God's demand,
Lest she protest and weep,
Insisting it must be Satan's work,
He who would never shirk
From seizing a little innocent child,
As his own gruesome perk.

So he took his son, a knife and some wood,
And two servants, well-trained from childhood.
They saddled their asses
And went on their way;
In silence they rode
Till the end of day.

Isaac, however, was much perplexed,
And asked Abraham, 'Dad, what's next?
I see the firewood and the knife,
But where's the lamb whose very life
Is to be offered to the Lord, our God —
Its absence, father, I find most odd!'

Abraham looked away from his son,
And tears flowed from his eyes:
'Have no fear, my precious one,
The lamb God always provides.

So they walked along, hand in hand,
Slowly traversing the hot desert sand;
Thoughts thrashing around in Abraham's head,
In Isaac's heart not a tincture of dread.

On the third day Abraham knew they'd arrived,
When he felt his spirits greatly revived;
And the presence of God –
It could not be denied –
He sensed profoundly,
By his side.

The two lads were deputed to bring
Heavy stones for the building
Of an altar compliant with God's desire
That Isaac, as sacrifice,
Be offered in fire.

The two were then told to return
Down the mount, lest they discern
What their master would perpetrate,
And lest, outraged, they attempt to frustrate
Isaac's God-ordained fate.

Abraham laid the wood on the altar of stone –
For what possible sin might this atone?
He took hold of Isaac and bound him firm,
But the lad did not so much as squirm,
Surrendering himself to the good Lord's grace,
Convinced that he would show his face
And deliver him out of that fearful place.

But Abraham focused on his task,
Reaching for the knife within his grasp;
Raising it aloft, ready to slay,
Granting himself just a moment's delay,
For the repose of his son's soul to pray:
'Let us both be united
In God this day!'

Suddenly, an angel's voice was heard,
'Stop, Abraham, you have grossly erred!
God never desired the life of your son;
It was but a trial of your faith – and you've won
The admiration of God and man –
Now leave this place as fast as you can!'

Abraham paused in utter confusion;
'Is this God's will or Satan's intrusion?
As the blood drained, his face turned pale.
'Was I summoned here then to no avail?
Would God have imposed such terrible pain
If there was no sacred purpose,
If all was in vain?

'At least let me wound him
In the chest or the thigh,
To silence my doubts
And my question, "Why?" '

'Put down your knife,
Do not graze his skin.
God has seen your devotion,
Your absence of sin;
That you would not withhold
What is dearest in life,
The only son of yourself
And Sarah, your wife.'

In the thicket beside him,
Abraham heard a stir;
A ram caught by its horns –
What did it augur?
'This must have been heaven's plan' –
So, in place of his son,
He offered up the ram.

The angel then spoke for a second time:
'Abraham is blessed of the divine;
His seed will increase like the stars of heaven,
So strong and secure
That none will dare threaten.'

## Death and burial of Sarah
### (23:1–2)

When Abraham returned to his home that night,
He was greeted by a fearful sight:
Crowds milled around his tent,
All to sorrow giving vent.

He suddenly felt so sad and old,
And guessed what had happened before being told:
Satan had reported to his delicate wife
That Abraham had taken young Isaac's life.
The shock that she suffered at the sound of that news –
And the thought that her husband was the accused –
Stopped her heart beating,
With grief suffused.

A hundred and twenty-seven
She was at her death;
She'd thanked the Lord,
With her dying breath:
For the life she'd shared with a partner so rare,
Whose faith in God was beyond compare;
For the child she'd born to continue the line,
And fulfil the mission that God would assign;
For the wayfarers, entertained in their tent,
For the respect they were shown wherever they went;
For the privilege of teaching the world God's truth –
Men and women, old folk and youth.

With a smile 'the princess' closed her eyes,
God's closeness her most cherished prize;
Israel's foremost matriarch,
Who'd leave on her people
An indelible mark.

## Purchase of Cave of Machpelah
### (23:3–20)

In Hebron where the Hittites ruled,
Sarah had breathed her last;
Permission to bury her on their soil
Abraham had to ask.

Their chief, Ephron – a wily man –
Refused to deal with strangers,
So Abraham, exceptionally,
Called in some past favours.

'I need your help,' he told some friends,
Who had previously sat at his table,
'To speak for me to your chief, Ephron,
If you feel that you're able.

'I wish to buy a burial plot
For the wife I have lost;
And I'm willing and able to pay in full –
Whatever that might cost.

'The two-layered cave at the edge of his land,
Will serve my purpose well;
I've silver coins of perfect mint,
If he's prepared to sell.'

The petition was relayed to Ephron
As he stood in the city gate,
About to disclose to his subjects
His parlous financial state.

'Let me meet that prince of God,'
Said he, 'before it's too late;
There's no time like the present,
So I mustn't let him wait!'

'Welcome, Abraham, my new dear friend,
I've been desperate to make your acquaintance.
Your petition is granted. Take it as a gift –
And that includes maintenance.'

Abraham bowed low to the ground,
'Lord Ephron, what can I say?
But a gift I really cannot accept –
For the cave I have to pay.'

'Very well,' said Ephron,
'Let's waste no more time;
The cave of Machpelah
Is a site truly prime.

'I had an offer yesterday,
From a group most financially sound,
To purchase not just the cave,
But the ground all around.

'I rejected the offer in my desire
To retain that family plot;
But if I now refused Your Eminence,
On my record it would be a blot.

'So I'll take a token – nothing more –
Four hundred silver shekel;
Though you and I know at the property mart,
T'would fetch at least treble.
And so that I'm not impoverished more,
Be so kind, my lord, as to ensure
That the coins are those that no merchant would void,
Pure silver in content,
Unalloyed.'

Abraham paid that exorbitant sum
Without so much as a word;
He buried his wife with tribute and prayer,
With his place next to hers reserved.

# A wife for Isaac
## (24:1–25:11)

One day Abraham summoned
The steward of his house,
Eliezer of Damascus –
Loyal to him and his late spouse.

'God has promised that I'd become
A great and holy nation;
But how can Isaac accomplish that
Without procreation?

'So, Eliezer, I charge you now
With finding for him a wife;
The girls of Canaan I've ruled out –
Their idolatry is rife.

'So return now to my family –
My own kith and kin –
Where you'll be sure to find a maiden
Wholly free of sin.

'But if you encounter difficulty
In discovering her whereabouts,
Be sure to seek God's guiding hand,
To remove any doubts.'

'But, master,' asked the servant true,
'What if the girl is unwilling to
Return with me to this Promised Land,
Am I still bound by your demand?'

'Indeed, you are, unequivocally;
So lay your hand upon my knee
And swear by the Lord of heaven above –
Who, throughout my life, has shown me love –
That you won't make my son return
To evil Chaldea,
The land I spurn.'

Eliezer gave his solemn oath,
And set out on his mission,
With ten camels and countless gifts –
Like a man of high position.

Arriving at the day's end,
He approached a local well;
Reining in his camels to give them drink,
He wondered if God would foretell
Which, of all the girls he could see,
Was the one chosen from above to be
Isaac's wife and a matriarch
To their future progeny.

'If, when I ask for water,
Not only does she comply,
But says, "I will also provide
For your camels a generous supply,"
Let that be the sign that she is the one
Chosen by you,
The Most High.'

It immediately became apparent
That God had answered his plea,
For the maiden replied in that identical way,
Filling him with ecstasy.

He presented her with costly gifts,
Two bracelets, a ring of gold.
He asked her name and if at her home
He could shelter from the cold.

'Rebecca, daughter of Betuel,'
She replied with a winsome smile,
'We've provisions for your animals,
And you may indeed stay awhile.

'You've travelled from Canaan –
That's clear for all to see –
Do you know my grandpa, Nahor
And Abraham's family?'

When he heard those words
Eliezer bowed down
In awe to the Lord above;
'Blessed be you,' he fervently cried,
'Who unites family in love.'

Just then, her brother Laban arrived –
A crafty, scheming man –
And seeing the camels and the gifts dispensed,
He immediately hit on a plan.

'Why, dear friend, are you standing outside?
Please repair to my humble abode,
To refresh yourself and eat your fill,
Before you commence to unload.'

A sumptuous meal was prepared for him,
But he refused to pick up a spoon:
'I cannot start till I've had my say –
I promise I'll eat soon.

'I'm the faithful servant of Abraham,
Brother of your and Rebekah's granddad;
God made my master a wealthy man,
Blessing everything he had.

'The apple of his eye, his son, Isaac,
Has yet to be wed.
When it comes to girls,
He's a retiring youth,
So he's sent me instead
To locate his heaven-sent twin-soul –
The crown of his head.

'God has led me to this place
And to your very home;
Meeting Rebekah, a girl unique –
I've no more need to roam.

'Let me take her back with me,
To become Isaac's wife;
She'll comfort him for the loss of his mum,
And brighten up his life.'

Brother Laban and her mum and dad
Looked long at Rebekah's gifts:
'O, forgive me,' said Eliezer,
'I've truly been remiss.
I've come with ten camels,
Bearing a dowry fit for a queen,
And rewards for you if you'll agree,
And if she herself is keen.'

'Of course I wish to marry
The great Prince Abraham's son' –
Interjected Rebekah –
'Whether or not he's handsome!'

So the matter was quickly concluded,
And Eliezer was wined and dined;
They toasted the two young people
Whose lives they'd just entwined.

To the gentle and pure Rebekah
They bade farewell next day,
Convinced that she would thrive
And be blessed in every way.

'Our beautiful daughter and sister' –
Their parting words rang out –
'Be the matriarch of countless tribes,
Whose enemies they shall rout.'

As the bridal cavalcade arrived
At Isaac's home in Ur,
He was praying in a nearby field,
And feeling quite unsure
Of the marital step he was about to take,
And of what would lie in store.

When Rebekah caught sight of him,
She covered her face with a veil;
He looked so distracted,
So sad and so pale.

Before long they were married,
And she occupied Sarah's tent.
Isaac's grief was assuaged
By a love that was heaven-sent.

Abraham took another wife,
Keturah was her name,
By whom he had six more sons –
All of whom gained fame.

He showered upon Isaac all he had,
And to each other son a bequest;
At a hundred and seventy five he died,
With one final request:

'Let my Ishmael be summoned
When I'm laid to rest;
I loved him dearly –
Let him know –
Though it was all for the best
That he lived his life
In his own way,
No faith in God professed.

Ishmael returned,
And the brothers embraced.
They buried their father
In the hallowed place
That he'd bought all those years before;
Joining Sarah at Machpelah
For evermore.

# Jacob and Esau
## (25:19–28)

Forty years old was Isaac
When he took Rebekah to wife;
But the years passed with no bundle of joy,
To light up their life.

They prayed each day,
They prayed each night;
They trusted in God
To relieve their plight.
In his own good time he granted their wish,
Putting an end to their anguish

Rebekah's stomach swelled so big –
Two little beings doing a jig –
But a deep foreboding seized the mother,
That one inside was pursuing the other.

She went to discern of the Lord, her God,
Why her emotions were so raw;
Why her offspring struggled so,
And what the future held in store.

*'Twin nations are in your womb,'*
The heavenly voice revealed.
*'But between them lies a rift so vast*
*That never will be healed.'*

The first of the babes to emerge
Had skin as red as blood;
Hairy as a woollen cloak,
With an even hairier hood.

*Esau,* they called him;
"Fully formed," was its import;
From birth the art of fighting
Seemed natural, self-taught.

His brother followed swiftly,
Grasping Esau's heel;
So they called him *Jacob* —
"One who pursues with zeal."

The boys grew up as different
As two brothers could possibly be;
Esau hunted the expanse between
The Jordan and the Sea.

He loved the chase,
He loved the shoot,
He loved the anguished cry
Of fleet-footed deer, felled in full-flight,
And the awe of passers-by.

Jacob was a man of simple tastes,
Rarely leaving his home.
He cooked and did the other chores,
And studied a large tome
That his grandpa, Abraham, had composed —
For their faith a corner-stone.

Esau's cunning knew no bounds;
When his dad was around he uttered the sounds
Of prayers he knew Isaac adored,
So that into him his father poured
All the hopes for the future
That he had stored.

## *Purchase of the birthright*
### (25:29–34)

One day, Esau missed his shot,
And the animal turned on him,
Knocking him roughly to the ground,
Dislocating a limb.

Esau limped home from the fight,
Painfully bemoaning his sorry plight;
Weary in body as well as in soul –
'My life-style,' he cried,
'Has taken its toll.'

As he staggered into the kitchen tent
He saw Jacob studiously bent
Over a pot exuding a delicious flavour,
Which Esau was suddenly desperate to savour.

'Share with me this divine red pottage:
Lentil stew with garlic and sausage.
There's nothing tastier, of which I can think –
Then I'll wash it down with a glass of strong drink.
This is a prisoner's final wish;
Brother, relieve me of my anguish.
Name your price,
Take all my estate –
But give me the stuff,
For I cannot wait!'

'I do have a price,' Jacob exclaimed;
'It's one which I've always claimed
Would come my way in the fullness of time,
To ensure that, when I reached my prime,
I'd inherit the firstborn's rightful estate –
Something to which you cannot relate!

'For, as you know, it's the firstborn's role
To observe to the letter Grandpa's scroll:
To make offerings to the God on high –
And never kill or cheat or lie –
To recite blessings over food,
And never utter a word that's crude;
To lead the family in daily prayer,
And perform acts of kindness everywhere.

'So, brother Esau, tell me true,
Do you really think that the likes of you
Would have been chosen as first-born,
To don priestly robes, with hair unshorn?
So let me buy that holy state –
And my stew shall make your hunger abate!'

'Brother, Jacob, an inspired offer!
I'm going to die so why should I bother
With who inherits the firstborn right?
Those sacred duties are remote from my sight.
I give you my oath;
You inherit the lot.
Just give me the stew –
I prefer the fleshpot.'

So the deal was struck,
And the oath delivered;
Esau went on his way –
But his goodwill soon withered.

# Isaac in adversity and prosperity
## (26:1–34)

Famine-prone Canaan,
With fields reduced to sand,
Drove Isaac to seek refuge
In Philistine land,
Where Abimelech welcomed him,
And the two warmly shook hands.

The king's eye alighted on his wife,
'What's she to you?' he enquired.
'She's my constant companion,
The joy of my life –
My sister!' Isaac replied.

One day, as they made passionate love,
The king, from his window, espied.
He summoned Isaac, demanding to know
The reason why he'd lied.

'In our family we value life –
For that we're rightfully famed;
Had I told you the truth, I have no doubt,
I'd be killed or seriously maimed.'

'You thoughtless one,'
Raged the king,
'To compromise your wife;
Bringing guilt upon my head,
And to my palace
Strife.'

The king issued a royal command
To his subjects far and wide,
To secure the safety of the man and his wife –
With all their needs supplied.

In the years that followed Isaac grew rich,
Gaining flocks in abundance;
His servants dug wells and water flowed,
Vastly increasing his substance.

But the men of Gerar, the capital city,
Marred his wells, showing no pity;
And when Isaac struck a deep-water course,
They filled it with boulders transported by horse.

Bitter feuding then broke out
Between the shepherds of each side;
So they named the wells "hatred" and "strife" –
Connoting claims that collide.

Isaac moved on to find some peace,
And dug another well;
They gave it the name *Rehovot*, "at ease,"
In the hope that now they might dwell
Together, as brothers, in common accord,
And misunderstanding dispel.

South to Beersheba was Isaac's next move,
New pastures to survey,
Where God appeared to him one night,
With a blessing to relay.

*'Fear not, my righteous Isaac,*
*I am ever by your side;*
*I will bless and multiply your seed,*
*So they prosper world wide.'*

Early next morning,
The sound of hoofs was heard;
Abimelech and his entourage,
Riding swiftly as a bird.

Isaac went out to meet him,
To determine his intent:
'Sir, what brings you here again;
On what mission are you bent?'

'Fear not, Prince Isaac,' said the king,
'In peace I approach;
What my men have done to you
Deserves severe reproach.

'To me it's as clear as the midday sun,
That God guides your every move;
So let's make a covenant of eternal peace,
Of which he would approve.'

They sat down together to a feast,
Professing a friendship that could only increase.
Abimelech repeated his good intent –
For the umpteenth time! –
Before he went.

So Isaac now had peace of mind,
No strife or skirmish of any kind;
To the surrounding tribes he now related –
But closer to home a new crisis waited!

## *Jacob, Esau and the birthright*
### (27:1–46)

Isaac was now advanced in years,
His eyesight was quite poor;
But his love for Esau was just as strong
As it was before.

One day he summoned him to his tent,
With a mission to fulfil:
'I'm old, my son; my strength is spent;
Indeed, I feel quite ill.
I'm no fool; I know the score:
Life can run its course,
And when that's done, the soul divine
Returns to its source.

'So do me one more favour, please,
My affairs I wish to leave
In good order,
With instructions clear
As to what my sons receive.

'Take now your bow, your arrow and sword;
To the field repair and hunt
A deer, and cook it as I love,
Piquant, not too pungent.

'Bring it to me to enjoy,
And my spirits will then soar;
And I will bless you as you deserve
With good things for evermore.

'But I won't leave your brother out –
For that would not be right –
Since God disclosed his destiny
To me just last night.'

Now Rebekah was standing outside his tent,
And she clearly overheard
And reported to Jacob, her adored son,
Isaac's every word.

'Now listen, Jacob, carefully,
To what I have to say;
However hard is my command,
Obey in every way.

'Go to the flock immediately,
And dispatch me two young goats.
I have in store a venison sauce
That would dupe most gourmets' throats.

'Esau's hunt will take him
At least till afternoon,
And by the time he's cooked the venison,
And polished a silver spoon,
You'll have gained your father's blessing,
Which none can then impugn!'

Jacob's face went pale with fear
And horror at his mother's words;
His throat became constricted,
As if bound by tight cords.

'But mother,' he finally whispered,
In a voice quaking and hoarse,
'At dad's embrace I'll be unmasked,
And the birthright he won't endorse.

'For my skin is soft and smooth,
And my brother's hairy and hard;
He'll curse me as a deceiver –
And with that I'll ever be tarred.
But if that is not harsh enough,
From the family I'll be barred.'

'Fear not, my son,' Rebekah soothed,
'You're blessed by the One Above;
Any curse I'll absorb,
And shield you with my love.

'Now, hurry and prepare his food;
These clothes of his now wear.
Tie on his boots
And roughen your hands
With goat's skin and hair.'

With trepidation Jacob set out
On his mission of deceit;
Entering into his father's room
With the "venison" for him to eat.

The whiff of the field that Isaac inhaled
Was in Esau's robe, to be sure;
But the silent tread of the sole of his foot,
Was a trifle too demure.

'Approach and let me assure myself
That you are Esau, the tough;
For though the voice is Jacob's,
The hands don't seem so rough!

'Which son are you?' he quizzed him,
'You have me quite confused,'
'What a question,' Jacob replied,
'I'm really not amused!'

'But how did you hunt the deer, my son,
With its venison slowly braised,
In just a couple of hours?' –
Asked his father, quite amazed.

'It was God who provided the deer, dad,
Ambling near our home;
He clearly wanted to see me blessed,
Rather than aimlessly roam.'

'Strange that Esau should invoke God!' –
The thought crossed Isaac's mind.
'I know he thought I was taken in
When, as a young child,
He'd loudly recite the sacred prayers
That he inwardly reviled!

'He thought I loved him for his faith,
For his gifts of meat and wine;
How far off the mark he was –
I love him because he's mine!

'But I must set all that on one side,
And cancel my erstwhile plan
To bless Esau with the firstborn's right
And make him head of the clan.

'For how can he dispense the task
Of preserving our sacred tradition,
And handing it down to posterity
As a uniquely spiritual mission?'

So he decided, there and then,
To withhold from *this son* his right,
And invest *the other* with all his estate,
Whatever strife that might incite.

But God stepped in to ensure
Jacob's vindication;
By erasing the intention of Isaac's mind
To confirm real Esau's station.

So Isaac relaxed, ate and enjoyed
The food of the son he thought he'd deployed
To put him in a frame of mind
To impart that blessing of a special kind.

He placed his hands on Jacob's head,
Closed his eyes and fervently said:
'May God grant you dew from heaven,
And the most fertile fields on earth;
May your corn and wine multiply seven
Times in volume and worth.

'May peoples acknowledge the skills you possess,
And nations the power that's yours;
Be lord and master over your brother,
And may he ever obey your laws.

'May they who curse you
In return be cursed,
And they who bless you
Be blessed.
That you are deserving of such reward
Has been divinely assessed.'

No sooner had Jacob made his way out
When Esau made his way in:
'Up you get, dad, and eat of my stew,
Then bless me
As one free of sin.'

'Who are you, my son? What is your name?'
Stuttered Isaac, his mind in torment.
'I'm Esau, your firstborn –
What's going on?
Who's that who just now went?'

Isaac's body shook like a reed,
'God must have arranged it,' he croaked;
'That was your brother;
He brought me food,
Dressed in your tunic and cloak.'

Esau uttered an ear-piercing shriek:
'A two-fold deception he's played;
He took advantage when I was weak,
And my birthright he made me trade.

'Now, by stealth, he's taken my blessing
And made me raving mad;
Surely father you'll agree
That what he's done is bad?
It cannot be the Lord God's wish
That he should steal all I had!'

'Oh, my son, you speak like a child.
God sees things as they are.
They cannot presume to fathom his mind
Who see things from afar.

'To you this looks just like deceit,
To me also it is not meet;
But I'm horrified that you approved
Of selling your birthright
In return for food!

God, who penetrates the heart,
And knows the end before the start –
His ways are just,
And we must bow
To his justice –
As you must now –
With courage and unfurrowed brow.
Indeed, you must,
Esau, my son,
Indeed, you must,
Right now.'

'It's easy for you, father mine;
For neither a protest nor a whine
Escaped your lips
When you were taken
To Moriah –
Quite forsaken.
Well I'm not one to lie down flat,
To be used as a doormat
By those who feather their own nest,
And don't give a shekel for the rest!

'I was the one you wanted to bless,
So, like your father, God address,
And demand of him to reverse
This situation
So perverse.'

'My son, that's not within my power,
Were I to pray every hour;
For God has sealed the blessing I gave –
In his eyes Jacob is no knave.
Now I've made him head of the clan,
With power over every man,
And blessed his corn and wine and oil –
And with abundance
All his soil.'

'Have you not one blessing left?
How can you leave me so bereft?'
Pleaded Esau,
Amid his tears –
Looking almost twice his years.

Isaac's heart went out to him,
He'd never known his mood so grim:
'My son, receive this blessing of mine –
Though it bears not the name divine:
May you inhabit places fair,
And pastures greened by dew;
Live by the sword and your brother protect,
And may all your troubles be few.
At a time to come –
I give my word –
You will, once more, arise,
And from your neck
His lordly yoke
You will forcefully prise.'

Esau's hatred knew no bounds,
And in his heart he swore
That after his father had quit this life,
He'd settle with Jacob the score.

He disclosed to a friend his murderous plan,
And the friend let Rebekah know;
She summoned Jacob and warned him
That it was time for him to go:

'Flee the family home at once,
Make sure you do not tarry;
To my brother, Laban's place repair –
And one of his daughters marry!

'A righteous partner is what you need,
In order to build our nation;
Just look at Esau's Hittite wives –
Our constant aggravation!'

Jacob went, that very eve,
To see the father he'd deceived:
'O father, dear, I'm so ashamed;
How can I make amends?
And now my brother wants me dead,
And I have so few friends.'

'Fear not, Jacob; it was God's plan.
Trust him as I've instilled,
Though I fear it was my blindness
That nearly got you killed.
'Now my eyes are open wide;
I see the Lord is on your side.
His plan for you he'll soon confide –
And brother Esau he won't abide.

'So off you go to Padan Aram,
To the home of our family there,
And may you find your destiny –
That is my fervent prayer.

'May you be blessed and multiplied
By the Lord God of Creation
Who promised your grandpa Abraham that
We'd become a great nation.'

# The dream of the ladder
## (28:10–22)

Jacob left, heavy of heart,
Hardly convinced that this was the start
Of a destiny that God would chart,
And of which he'd be an active part.

After a full day's ride at a speedy pace,
He alighted at an eerie place;
With its awesome aura he felt embraced,
And overawed by holy space.

Jacob sensed he wasn't alone,
But was being observed;
He prayed to God and prepared for sleep,
Considerably unnerved.

He took twelve stones as a support
For his heavy, distracted head;
He smoothed the ground
And then lay down
On his makeshift bed.

After a while he closed his eyes,
And soon began to dream
Of a ladder reaching to the skies,
And, caught in a moonbeam,
Angels gliding up and down –
A translucent celestial team.

Above the ladder, in a haze, he saw…
Who else could it be?
He was constrained to avert his gaze,
Instinctively.

*Jacob, be not afraid*
*Of what you've just seen.*
*Offspring of Abraham, my friend,*
*And Isaac whom I esteem —*
*This place where you have your dream,*
*In holiness is supreme.*

*'In time to come, on this site,*
*My temple shall stand as a beacon of light.*
*Nations shall come and acclaim your worth —*
*And you'll be abundant as the dust of the earth.*

*'Fear not what the future may bring,*
*For I determine everything;*
*To Canaan, one day, you'll return,*
*And there your offspring shall sojourn.*
*As for the angels going up and down —*
*Your deeds have created for them a crown —*
*The first watched over you till this day,*
*The rest descend to smooth your way.'*

Jacob awoke from his sleep,
Not knowing whether to laugh or weep;
'God's never appeared to me before,
And here, lying on the floor,
I'm vouchsafed a wondrous revelation
That I'll become a great nation.
How did I deserve to locate
The house of God
And heaven's gate?'

Next morning, in the terrain,
There was no trace of where he'd lain.
And the twelve stones he'd arranged,
Into one large slab had now been changed!
He anchored it firmly into the soil,
And poured over it anointing oil.
'*Beth El* is the name it shall now be called,

God's house forever I've just installed;
And when I return to my land,
Accept, Lord, tithes
From the toil of my hand.'

## *Approaching Laban's home*
### (29:1–12)

Emboldened now and charged with elation,
He rode east with determination.
Arriving at the central well,
He asked the shepherds if they could tell
Him where he might locate a man
Called Laban –
They replied, 'We can!'

'In fact,' said one, 'here comes his daughter,
The gorgeous Rachel, to draw her water,
To quench the thirst of her father's flock –
But she'll have to wait till the dead-weight rock
That covers the well is lifted by us
Three shepherds together, without much fuss;
Then, when we've watered our own sheep,
We'll let the girls approach –
And we'll take a peep!'

'Be off with you!' said Jacob amazed,
'The sun's still high in the sky;
So the flocks have plenty more time to graze –
Their full quota you scoundrels deny!'

Just as the shepherds, in anger, rose
To give Jacob a thorough beating,
He whipped the rock off the top of the well –
And the lambs all started bleating.

The shepherds fell back in dismay
At the amazing strength on display;
At the uplifted rock
They abandoned their flock –
And in total panic
Ran away.

When Rachel approached
Jacob instinctively knew
That this was the love of his life;
That she was the one who was heaven-sent
To be his partner and wife.

He gave her sheep to drink their fill,
And then replaced the rock;
They talked and embraced until
Their love was soon unlocked.
He planted a kiss on her cheeks
And wept tears of joy,
'To find you I have travelled weeks;
There's no need to be coy!
I am your cousin, after all –
Your aunt Rebekah's boy!

'Just beware,' said Rachel,
'For my father can't be trusted.
Take every promise that he makes
With a couple of seeds of mustard!'

## Jacob at Laban's home
### (29:13–30:13)

When Laban was told that Jacob had come,
The potential for gain made him run
To greet the young man with a warm embrace –
But the smile was soon wiped off his face!

'When your grandpa's servant arrived here,
Many years ago,
He came laden with many gifts –
But you with a mere *hello!*'

'Forgive me, uncle that I don't impress,
For a fugitive am I;
Let me work on your estate,
Rather than just stand by.'

A month passed, and Laban saw
That Jacob was there to stay;
'You can't work here for nothing, lad –
That is not our way!'

In Laban's mind a plan was hatched:
Older daughter, Leah, was not yet matched.
Her face was sallow, her figure narrow;
Her eyes weak, she didn't much speak;
Always looked tired,
Was never admired;
No wonder no suitors
Had enquired.

'Jacob, good fellow, you need a wife,
And I know for whom you care;
So for how long are you prepared to work?
Let's agree a term that's fair.'

'Indeed, I love her,' Jacob replied,
'And Rachel loves me too;
Is seven years a fair bride's price?
I think so;
Don't you?'

His love for her was so intense,
Time passed like a few days;
The nuptials arranged,
The townsfolk came,
To shout their *hurrays*!

Heavily veiled,
To the canopy
The bride was conveyed;
And when the last guest had gone,
The bridal bed was made.
In the deep darkness of the night
The couple were united;
But when the morning light shone in,
Jacob's hope was blighted.
For, lying next to him,
Was not the one he adored,
But her homely sister, Leah –
Whom he'd hitherto ignored.

He rushed straight to Laban's tent,
Beside himself with rage;
Denouncing him for the treachery
In which he'd been engaged.

'In the light of what you've done to me,
Can I go after Leah a-wooing?
Demonstrating passion for
A conspirator in my undoing?'

'Come, Jacob,' Laban replied,
'I'm surprised you don't know
That life has an inexorable rule
That we reap what we sow;
Did you not supplant your older brother,
And secure his birthright under cover?
But in *our* place we don't stoop so low
As to leave the older in limbo!

'But just to show my good intent,
Once this week's celebration's spent,
I'll give you Rachel as you desired –
If for seven more years
You agree to be hired!'

True to his word, the marriage took place,
And Laban allotted a suitable space
On his estate for the new families created;
And his generosity was not belated:
A maid, Zilpah, to Leah he allocated,
And on Rachel, Bilhah, dutifully waited.

The Lord was not pleased that Leah was hated,
So he blessed her with children to be more rated.
Reuben, the firstborn, was the joy of her life,
And she was now accounted
A fully-fledged wife.

Simeon, Levi and Judah
Followed in quick succession;
Leah's nest now became
Jacob's proudest possession.

Rachel grew more bitter
With each passing day;
Though Jacob sought to console her
In every possible way.

'Give me children,' she would cry.
'Without them I shall surely die.
That such a gift is yours to supply
Is a fact you cannot deny.
For it is abundantly clear to me
That you and God speak;
Yet now, when I've a desperate need,
You act incredibly meek!'

Jacob flew into a rage,
Though by nature mild.
'Do I stand in place of God
Who withholds from you a child?'

Rachel paused for awhile,
Then she had a thought:
'With my handmaid, Bilhah, as a wife
Would you now consort?
If you do,
The child produced
Would fulfil my maternal need,
And I would be fulfilled, my love;
Of my burden I'd be freed.'

Jacob lay with the maid,
And in the course of time,
A son, Dan, was born to them,
Meaning 'God has "judged" my crime –
In speaking out and laying blame
On Jacob, a righteous man,
Who mercifully has now confirmed
His pleasure at my plan.'

The second child the maid produced,
Was Naphtali, "my desperation,"
Recalling Rachel's jealousy
At her sister's propagation.

When Leah saw she was bearing no more,
She gave Jacob Zilpah, her maid.
Gad and Asher arrived,
And Leah thrived
On the love Jacob newly displayed.

## Reuben and the Mandrakes
### (30:14–24)

Reuben took an unfamiliar path,
During the harvest's aftermath,
When he saw some mandrakes on the ground –
A plant he'd never previously found.

An old man, a passer-by,
Watched him examine his find;
'That plant's not for the likes of you –
It's of a special kind.'

'What do you mean,' demanded the lad,
'By "a special kind"?
If you don't explain to me in full,
You'll get a piece of my mind!'

'As you will,' replied the man,
'But I suspect you might blush:
To embrace any woman who eats this plant
There's not a man won't rush.
He'll find no way for himself to cool
The ardour of his loins –
And a conception is guaranteed
When with her he joins.'

To Leah, his mum,
Reuben brought his find;
But when Rachel entered,
Leah read her mind:
'Be content you enjoyed
All our husband's passion;
Don't think now to acquire
This extra ration!'

'Then sell me your mandrakes,' Rachel implored,
'For an extra night with our husband adored.'
The deal was struck,
The mandrakes exchanged;
And Leah joined Jacob –
As arranged.

Issachar was conceived thereby,
Then Zevulun, always shy;
Finally, Dinah, a beautiful girl,
Viewed by Leah as her precious pearl.

Just when Rachel had given up hope,
God banished her gloom:
In answer to her fervent prayers
He opened up her womb.
This child, Joseph, was clearly blessed
With double the beauty of the rest.

## *Farewell to Laban's home*
### (30:25–32:3)

Years had passed and Jacob longed
To return to his home and land;
To let his aged parents bask
In the pleasure now at hand.

But life in Canaan he knew was hard,
And he'd need to build from scratch;
So he approached Laban one bright day
With a plan that he'd hatched.

'Sir, you know how hard I've worked,
Not making a single demand;
Well now the time I feel is right
To return to my land.

'My aged parents must certainly wish
To see before they die
The young son whom they always viewed
As the apple of their eye;
And to dandle on their knee
Grandchildren they must pine to see,
And reap family joys galore –
I ask you that – and nothing more.'

Laban looked none too pleased,
Suspecting Jacob's guile;
He feared he might, over the years,
Have decided to stockpile
Some of his master's valuables
For a future grand lifestyle.

'My condition for agreeing to this
Is absolutely clear;
I know that since you've worked for me
You've lived the life austere;
You've brought much blessing to my home –
That cannot be denied –
And I'd be considered ungrateful
If you weren't generously supplied.

So determine what I owe you,
And that in full I'll pay;
But take not another stitch
With you on the way.'

'You have a deal,' said Jacob,
'And for the wages that I seek,
Let me select from your flocks
Some animals that are weak.

'You'll recognise the ones I mean,
Speckled, spotted and dark;
The sort that even Noah
Wouldn't admit to his ark!'

Jacob proceeded to remove
The kind that they'd agreed;
His sons led them three days away,
To pastures new to feed.

Jacob then tried his hand
At some old fertility tricks:
Poplar, almond and plane-tree rods
He scraped down to their white strips.

He set them in the watering troughs,
When Laban's flocks came to drink;
And the sight and feel of those rods
Made a symbiotic link.

The result of this encounter
Was that those sheep gave birth
To speckled and spotted offspring –
Augmenting Jacob's worth.

The sons of Laban grew jealous
Of Jacob's vast herd:
'By means of some witchcraft
He's gone and altered
The natural balance of the flocks
So they're mostly striped and dark;
And dad is bereft of all his wealth,
While Jacob's made his mark.'

Jacob also noticed
A change in Laban's mood;
He was distinctly cool towards him,
If not overtly rude.

Jacob disclosed to his wives one day,
That the time had come to run away:
'Your dad, when reviewing my situation,
Has determined to keep me a poor relation.

He also revealed that God had appeared
In a dream the previous night,
To confirm the time to leave had come,
For his destiny was now in sight.

Rachel and Leah were not surprised
At what their husband had said:
'He never gave us a single gift,
That miserly hard-head!
And whatever blessing, substance and wealth
Your efforts generated –
Father always found some major fault
For which you were berated.'

While Laban was absent shearing his sheep,
Rachel stole a small idol he'd kept,
To which he prayed before going to sleep,
To protect him while he slept.

Jacob's family made good their escape,
Keeping a distance of three days,
Lest Laban pursue and frustrate
The plans they'd carefully laid,
And retrieve the speckled and spotted flocks
For which Jacob hadn't paid.

When Laban heard of Jacob's flight,
He sought that mighty wrong to right;
In hot pursuit off he went,
Riding till his strength was spent.

The night before the confrontation
God came to Laban in a dream:
*'I'll not resort to equivocation –*
*Righteous Jacob I esteem.*
*His flight without notification*
*You consider an unworthy act,*
*But there are ten examples of your reneging*
*On a solemn pact.*
*So I hereby give you the clearest warning*
*Against attempting any harm.*
*The scores are settled,*
*A new day's dawning –*
*Speak to him, but remain calm.'*

At Mount Gilead their paths converged,
And Laban's anger soon emerged:
'You kidnapped my daughters like captives of war,
Not a single gift from my store
Could I bestow, not even a kiss
For them and the grandchildren I would miss.
But worse than that, how could you steal
My gods that bless, protect and heal?'

Jacob, shocked by that allegation,
Proceeded to offer protestation:
'I worked for you for twenty years,
Fourteen for your daughters and six for my herds.
Your ewes and goats never miscarried,
The sum of your flocks always tallied;
From my purse I replaced those gored by wild beasts,
Not one of your sheep did I use for my feasts;
In winter I suffered the cold and the frost,
Not a single day through illness was lost.
In the height of summer, with the sun on my head,
I never left my post, even to break bread.
And as for this charge that your gods I have taken,
Soon to the truth you'll surely awaken.'

Laban proceeded to search Jacob's camp,
In confined spaces, even using a lamp;
But not one idol could he locate,
So his anger steadily began to abate.

On his return he asked Rachel why
She hadn't stood up when her father passed by;
For she'd sat on a camel's saddle bag,
Wherein was the idol, wrapped in a rag!

'Forgive me, father,
But my period's arrived,
And this seat gives me comfort –
It's soft and well-piled.'

By this simple act of retribution,
Rachel made her father pay
For his callous act of substitution
Of Leah on her wedding day.

So Laban and Jacob were reconciled
And made a peace accord;
Setting up a pillar to assert
That they'd never wield the sword.
And Jacob promised that he'd cherish
Laban's daughters in every way,
And would never replace them for another
Up until his dying day.

After Laban bade farewell,
Jacob encountered on his march
A vast camp of guardian angels –
Protection with Esau at large.

## Jacob and Esau's reunion
(32:4–24)

He wasn't reassured by this vision,
Knowing Esau's disposition,
Especially when his scouts announced in due course
That four hundred men were in Esau's force.
They were also unclear as to his intention –
Whether revenge or reconciliation.

Jacob was gripped by a terror –
Not that his faith was in error;
It was rather that he might come to slay
His own brother in the fray.

His second approach was diplomatic,
If a trifle enigmatic:
Sending servants to petition
Esau and express contrition.

'Your servant Jacob' – they told Esau –
'His life has been just like a see-saw;
Fleeing from your noble presence,
Encountering angels and God's essence.

'Then he entered Laban's household,
Where he worked for twenty years;
Strong in body, strong in spirit,
A man of faith, devoid of fears.

'Asses, camels, sheep and cattle –
Of his wealth all townsmen prattle –
With countless monarchs of the East
He's signed treaties of permanent peace,
Agreeing to offer whatever aid
Was needed to repulse a raid.

'But Jacob seeks no confrontation,
Only reconciliation,
For which reason these gifts are proffered
And the hand of friendship firmly offered.'

Three waves of servants Jacob sent,
To make quite clear his good intent;
And hundred of beasts as a gift,
To heal past wounds and remove the rift.

These were all sent on ahead;
With darkness as cover, Jacob led
His family across the Jabbok river,
Returning for his arrow and quiver.

## Wrestling with the Angel
### (32:25–33)

He slept alone in his camp that night,
But was awakened by a fearful sight:
An angelic warrior stood close by,
With a menacing look in his eye.

Jacob rose and the two locked arms,
Fighting, wrestling, straining palms,
Pulling, wrenching shoulder and back,
With the thrust and parry of each attack.

The whole night long, in struggle and tussle,
They pummelled each other and stretched every muscle.
His assailant couldn't subdue his foe,
So he retreated an instant, feigning to go,
Then, just as Jacob lowered his guard,
The angel lunged with a blow so hard
That it dislocated Jacob's thigh,
Though he still clung on,
With a muffled cry.

His adversary, seeing that day had dawned,
Was struck with fear, for he'd been warned
By the angel Michael that he mustn't delay,
But return on high in time to pray.
'Let me go. I must sing the Lord's praise,'
He begged, with arms submissively raised.

'If you are all Esau could muster,
Then I'm not impressed by all your bluster.
Confirm me in the firstborn's right,
And confer its blessing on me this night.'

The angel, thereupon, asked his name,
Then announced that he was no longer the same
Jacob who'd grasped his brother's heel,
But was now the father of 'Israel' –
Meaning, one who wrestles with God and man,
And prevails in a way none other can.

Jacob called the place, 'Peniel,'
Meaning, 'Face of God,'
So that his offspring might remember
This episode most odd.

For, when he tried to move from there,
He limped in his stride;
Hence, Hebrews won't eat, in an animal,
The thigh muscle of that side.

# *The Jacob-Esau encounter*
## (33:1–17)

Jacob, his sons and four wives,
Bowed seven times as they went;
Hoping and praying, with hearts beating fast,
That Esau's anger was spent.

When Esau caught sight of his brother ahead,
No vestige of vengeance remained in his head;
His heart melted and from his eyes there sprung
Tears of joy, and to Jacob he clung.

They vowed that they'd make a new start,
Avoiding the issues that had kept them apart;
Esau received the gifts as a brotherly token
Of the dawn to which they had newly woken.

In Shechem Jacob settled down,
On land he'd bought at the edge of the town.
He now looked forward to peace of mind,
To the calm and comfort of the kind
That had eluded him throughout his life –
But on the horizon there loomed further strife!

# *Dinah*
## (34:1–31)

Dinah was the talk of the men of Shechem,
From the curve of her figure to the length of her hem.
While all the other girls took a chaperone,
She preferred to wander around town alone.

A free spirit, she was warned by her dad
That, among the young men, were some who were bad;,
And a girl who cherished her reputation
Had to be wary of association,
Maintaining, at all times, discrimination.

But Dinah just smiled and blew dad a kiss,
Assuring him that nothing would go amiss.
I can't just cook and feed the sheep,
Or chat to my brothers and then go to sleep!'

Dinah was accepted by the Shechemite girls,
And at their dances was famed for her twirls.
Shechem, son of Hamor, the chief of that city,
Flirted with Dinah, the new girl so pretty.

But Dinah knew that her father's clan
Would accept no liaison with a local man.
But the more she refused Shechem's advances,
The more he ogled her at the dances.
One night he followed her without a sound,
And, on her way home, pushed her to the ground.

He had his way with Dinah,
Who cried to no avail;
He told her that he loved her

And begged her not to wail;
For she was an adult, no longer a child,
And must not feel, in any way,
That she had been defiled.

'My love for you is greater now
Than ever it was before;
Don't imagine for a moment
I regard you as a whore.
The very opposite is the truth –
I'd lay down for you my life,
And pay the highest bride-price
To claim you as my wife.

Dinah was so confused
By what Shechem had said;
Conflicting thoughts about him
Jostled in her head.
She knew that her father,
And her grandpa too,
Had been warned most sternly
Against attempting to woo
Anyone from Canaan –
However fine in their view.

But then she had another thought:
No suitor now would ever be sought
By her father from Laban's kin,
So would it really be a sin
If she wed Shechem, a local man,
And future leader of his clan?

So she acceded to his request
That she return to his home and take a rest
While an approach to her father was formally framed,
And a convenient date for the wedding named.

Unknown to Shechem, one of his foes,
Seeing Dinah dishevelled, ran to disclose
To Jacob and sons her most unfortunate plight,
And that the poor girl had looked such a sight!
He wasn't slow to proclaim his view
That their poor Dinah had lost her virtue!

The family was shocked by what it heard,
That to their Dinah such a thing had occurred;
And when Hamor came to present his petition,
They noted the absence of any contrition.

He was clearly intent to gloss over the deed,
As if these Hebrews were an inferior breed
That could be bought off with some sheep or ewes,
Or some larger inducement they couldn't refuse.

'Jacob, dear friend,' Hamor began,
'With joy in my heart and a matrimonial plan,
I come to help you integrate
Into this, my land, and initiate
An enterprise of mutual gain,
Enhancing our illustrious name.

'Your Dinah has won the heart of my son,
And when these negotiations are done,
We'll escort her back in princely style –
Forgive us that we've detained her awhile!

'Let this be the start of a deepening bond
Between two clans who will become so fond
Of each other as the years unfold,
With marriages yielding kindred untold.
But, for now, let us both share much joy
From Dinah, your daughter, and Shechem our boy.'

A pregnant silence hung in the air;
On Jacob's face a look of despair.
The brothers retired to consider the matter,
Leaving father Jacob idly to chatter.

Simeon and Levi presented the case:
'They are too numerous for us to face
In conventional battle, man against man;
So listen carefully to our ingenious plan.

'We'll appear to accept the marriage deal,
On condition that they agree to seal
Within their flesh the circumcision –
Sign of great grandpa Abraham's mission.

'Then, when they're weak from the knife,
We'll fall on them and take their life;
Revenge for Shechem's insensitivity
In presuming to steal Dinah's virginity.'

They returned and gave Hamor the news
That they saw much merit in his views;
Subject to that one stipulation,
That they be circumcised like the Hebrew nation.

On the third day,
As the Shechemites lay
Weak on their beds
And unfit for a fray,
Simeon and Levi each drew his sword,
And, making common accord,
Went through every Shechemite tent,
Slaying each male as they went.
Venting their outrage on them all,
For the rape of their sister,
After the ball.

The other brothers followed behind,
Seizing booty of every kind:
Flocks, herds, weapons and flagons,
Wives and children, asses and wagons.
They found Dinah, in shock and grief
At all the violence, and in disbelief
That she, God-fearing Jacob's daughter,
Had been the cause of all that slaughter.

They took her back to her father in tears,
But he was preoccupied with other fears:
'Simeon and Levi, you deserve a curse.
You've blackened my name –
But even worse,
When the Canaanite clans hear of your deed,
They'll determine to annihilate us and our seed.
We are so very few in number,
Now *we'll* be the victims of violence and plunder.'

'Father,' the two brothers replied,
'What the future will bring, God will decide;
But he must have had retribution in store,
For those who made of our sister a whore.'

# Death of Rachel
## (35:16–20)

While Esau's clan spread abroad –
Putting many to the sword,
Seizing lands in quick succession,
With Mount Seir their prime possession –
Jacob's family never moved
From Canaan, the land
That God approved.
But Jacob lost the love of his life:
On the road to Ephrat, Rachel his wife
Writhed in pain upon the earth
Attempting to expel a premature birth.

As she felt her strength ebbing away,
And heard the cries of her child's first day,
She called him Ben Oni, "son of my sorrow,"
But Jacob, looking beyond the morrow,
Named him Benjamin, "my right-hand man,"
Who'll comfort my old age as much as he can.

He buried her near Bethlehem,
Erecting a pillar over her grave;
Lamenting that her resting-place
Was not Machpelah's cave.

*But that loyal and selfless sister,*
*Who'd kept silent when replaced,*
*Would come to occupy a niche,*
*That would never be displaced,*
*As an eternal symbol*
*Of a people set aside,*
*Deceived and degraded,*
*With their national rights denied.*

*But Rachel's tears — it was believed —*
*Together with her prayers,*
*Would secure an end to Israel's woes,*
*And calm her nation's cares.*

## Reuben and Bilhah
### (35:22)

Though Reuben was the firstborn
He feared a rival claim,
And worried now, with Rachel gone,
That her maid, Bilhah, might attain
Her mistress's place as chief wife
With its attendant gain.

Then she might press for one of her sons
To lead the other tribes;
Creating a dynasty of handmaids
Replacing that of wives.

But, versed in the laws of the Canaanites,
Reuben thwarted her plan;
He lay with Bilhah one dark night,
And thus became her man;
No longer permitted
To Jacob as a wife,
She'd become Reuben's handmaid
At the close of Jacob's life.

Jacob was incensed at Reuben's gross deed:
'Why has God punished me with such rebellious seed?
What was Reuben's motive?' He asked himself each day,
'And why abase Bilhah in that unseemly way?'

But when the truth dawned
That Reuben feared a Bilhah plot,
To secure the birthright for her son –
He blushed and grew quite hot.
For that is just what he had done
At his mother's instigation;
So who was he now to express
Such righteous indignation?

But the thought of all around him
Manipulating his life,
Made him recall once again
His sorely missed wife –
Rachel, that one for whom
His love was paramount,
And who, until her dying day,
Had hurdles to surmount.

Even in death her fate was cruel,
And her peace of mind impaired;
Denied her place in Machpelah,
With an eternity to be shared.
Instead, it was Leah
Who would supplant her as before,
And lie with him in that hallowed cave –
Yoked for evermore!

What could he do for Rachel,
To redress her perennial pain,
And restore the balance of justice
By limiting Leah's gain?

In a flash, he saw it clearly;
Leah's Reuben would pay dearly.
For humbling Bilhah to gain succession –
He'd lose the firstborn's prized possession.

Judah was the natural choice
To replace him as the chief;
But in Rachel's son, Joseph,
He'd far greater belief.

## *Joseph*
(37:1–3)

An abundance of attributes
Set Joseph apart,
But his father loved him best of all
For his qualities of heart.

A son of Jacob's old age,
Always by his side;
His every meal and comfort
Joseph would provide.

While the other sons had married,
With children of their own –
Feeding the large family flocks
And running their home –
Joseph had all the time
To meditate and dream,
And imbibe father's wisdom
Which flowed like a stream.

Joseph was endowed
With a beauty most rare,
When he walked into town,
Folk would stop and stare
At his stature so erect and his graceful gait,
His flowing curls, shoulder length,
And his robes, well-cut, ornate.

But his doting father, Jacob,
When he gazed at Joseph's face,
Just saw his lovely Rachel,
Her beauty and her grace;
And all the love and longing,
Harboured in his heart, now torn,
He directed toward Joseph,
From the day that he was born.

Reflecting on that tragic loss,
Jacob made up his mind:
Within the tribal legacy
That he would leave behind,
There'd be a double portion
For Joseph to divide,
As recompense to Rachel
For all she'd been denied.

But there was more to Joseph
Than Jacob could define:
He sensed God had invested him
With power to divine
Precisely what was heaven's plan
In any situation –
A prophet and a statesman,
Mature in calculation.

For all of these attributes,
He invested Rachel's son
With a coat of many colours,
Exquisitely spun
By the tailor whom all
The local chiefs deputed
To provide their cloaks of office,
As convention instituted.

The sons of Leah moved
From envy to despair,
Their displacement by Joseph
Was more than they could bear:
A tragic re-run of a parental disposition
To brush aside the firstborn's right
To his paramount position.

'Has father learnt nothing
From his grandpa Abraham's strife
At banishing from his home
Hagar, his lesser wife,
And from the fact that Ishmael,
Still bridling at the hurt,
To ambush and attack us
Is ever on alert?

'And has he not forgotten the fear and the dread
That he himself suffered because, instead
Of accepting heaven's chronology of birth,
He invested the firstborn blessing
With pecuniary worth?

'And now, once again, he has nullified the norm,
And elevated Joseph, thus creating a storm
That will, doubtlessly, reverberate down the ages,
Breeding ill-will between our tribes
And mystifying sages.'

# Joseph's Dreams
## (37:4–11)

Now Joseph could not conceal
The contents of his heart;
And a pastoral dream he had one night
Was really the start
Of a most bitter feud that finally
Set him and his brothers apart.

'Brothers, we were binding sheaves
Of corn in the heat of the day,
When my sheaf stood erect
And summoned yours its way.
Your sheaves then surrounded mine
And made a low prostration,
Like courtiers before a king –
To confirm my elevation.'

The brothers stared, visibly shocked;
Pent up emotions were swiftly unlocked:
'Is it kingship now that you desire,
And all our possessions to acquire?
How smug you appear in your coloured attire,
As if you were a rose and we the briar.'

Yet another dream Joseph dreamt,
And to all the family he immediately went:
'Sun and moon and eleven stars,
Last night, by God, were sent
To bow before me and fulfil
The full divine intent.'

Jacob, witnessing the brothers' hate,
Could hold his peace no more:
'Joseph, is it appropriate
To lay such strife in store?

'For who is the sun and who the moon,
And the eleven stars so bright,
If not the family wherein you were reared,
Which you now so thoughtlessly slight?'

Desperate to calm the situation,
Jacob sent the brothers away,
To feed the flocks in a fertile location
Near Shechem, with instructions to stay.

## Kidnapping and sale of Joseph
### (37:12–36)

Some time later Jacob heard
Of regional battles brewing.
He was naturally most concerned
As to how his sons were doing.

He summoned Joseph and told him to go
To Shechem without delay,
To determine their safety and that of the sheep,
And how they had fared with their stay.

Joseph took a wrong turn,
And wandered to and fro.
A passer-by questioned him
As to where he wished to go.

'I'm looking for my brothers,
Ten shepherds in a group.'
'Ah,' said the man, 'I heard them say:
"To Dotan let us troop".'

Off went Joseph and saw them there;
He waved from afar.
'Here comes the dreamer,' they all cried,
'Not so lucky now, his star!'

'Come, let's kill him,' one of them said,
With which most of the others concurred,
'Or cast him into one of the pits,
Where his cries won't be heard.'

Reuben was about to rush away
To grandpa Isaac's funeral that very day.
For years immune to those around,
That sage hadn't uttered a single sound.
So Reuben went off to represent the rest,
And deliver a tribute which he could do best.

But Reuben's conscience smote him
At the brothers' ugly scoffing,
And at the threat of violence
That was clearly in the offing.

He was also in no doubt
As to whom his dad would blame
For not protecting Joseph
From mishap or pain.

'I've hurt my father several times,
But if I save Joseph now,
Perhaps he'll forgive my shortcoming
And restore my rank somehow.'

So he decided that, on his return,
He'd raise Joseph from the pit,
And bring him back to his father's home,
All safe, secure and fit.

After he left, the brothers all
Wasted no time at their task,
Stripping Joseph of his coloured coat,
They mockingly asked:
'What has become, Your Majesty,
Of all those exalted dreams?
That you've mistaken their import
Is clearly how it seems!'

They threw him into the empty pit,
Ignoring all his pleading;
Taunting him mercilessly down the shaft,
With gestures and blaspheming.

Satisfied with what they'd done,
They sat down to take a snack,
And watched a trading caravan
Of Ishmaelites coming back
From Gilead where they'd stocked up
With spices and perfumes
To sell in Egypt, and, in return,
To buy corn and choice legumes.

Judah turned to his brothers,
And shared with them his view:
'What will we gain by killing him;
No money will accrue?
Better sell him to these Ishmaelites –
He's our brother after all –
We'll at least share some proceeds,
And continue to walk tall.'

So they flagged down the caravan
And concluded a deal;
Twenty silver coins Joseph fetched –
Then they finished off their meal!

The Ishmaelites stopped over
At an inn for a couple of nights,
Where they, in turn, sold Joseph
To some Midianites
Who were also making for Egypt
To sell the wares they'd bought –
Where they sold Joseph to Potiphar,
Chief steward of Pharaoh's court.

Meanwhile, all the brothers
Agreed an alibi –
A cunning deception
And a calculated lie.
They tore his many-coloured coat,
Dipped it in sheep's blood,
And sent it to their father,
Overlaid with mud.

The messengers that they sent
Were told to declare
That they'd come across his son's coat
Near a lion's lair.

'Is this the coloured coat, sir,
That belonged to your son?
If so, we have to tell you
He's been violently undone.'

Tears streaming down his face,
Jacob stroked the tattered lace:
'My son, my son,' he wailed aloud,
'You, of whom I was so proud,
Son of Rachel, my adored wife,
I'll mourn you, Joseph,
Till the end of my life.'

— ❧❧ —

# *Judah and Tamar*
## (38:1–30)

Their father's grief brought about
Some bitter recriminations;
But it was mainly against Judah
That they levelled protestations.

'You were the one
Whose orders we obeyed.
When we sold our brother,
Had you but once said:
"Take him back to father,
He's had sufficient fright,"
Our consciences would now be clear
And father's spirits bright.'

Hurt by their denunciation
And self-righteous allegation,
Judah one day upped and left,
Leaving the family doubly bereft.

In Adullam, a Canaanite city,
He married a girl, headstrong and pretty.
Er and Onan came in quick succession,
Both sons prone to aggression.
Twenty years on, when the family had thrived,
Shelah, unexpectedly arrived.

Judah found a wife for Er,
Called Tamar, a local beauty;
But God struck him down before
He'd performed his marital duty.

So Judah instructed Onan
To take his late brother's wife;
To perpetuate – as was the norm –
The deceased brother's life.

Most grudgingly Onan agreed,
Since he knew full well that any seed
Would preserve the spirit of the one who'd died,
Reducing his own parental pride.

So, he lay with Tamar that first night,
But withheld from her the conjugal right;
Ensuring she did not conceive,
Humiliating her and making her grieve.

This act God could not abide,
It marred the sanctity of a bride;
So, as with Er, he slew Onan –
Leaving Tamar a widow
In Judah's clan.

Local law was very clear:
Little Shelah was the next 'levir',
He was the one who, by right,
Must marry Tamar, the Canaanite.

But Judah feared for the life of his son,
For Shelah was now his only one:
'Tamar, return to your father's home,
Until the time when Shelah is grown
Old enough to make you his own.'

But the years passed, and Tamar waited,
While Judah clearly procrastinated.
Tamar feared that further delay,
To motherhood would block her way.

Even later, after Judah's wife died,
Tamar's petition remained denied.
No word of marriage was ever spoken –
And her bruised spirit was now wholly broken.

That Spring, when Judah went sheep-shearing,
At Timnah in the hills,
Tamar hatched an audacious plan
To cure all her ills.

Taking off her widow's dress,
She concealed herself with a veil,
And raced on ahead of him,
Over hill and dale.
Posing as a harlot
In an open space,
She invited Judah to approach
And to enjoy her grace.

Outside the town of Einayim,
Alone in that desolate place,
Judah was enticed to take the girl
Knowing he wouldn't lose face.

'I'd sleep with you,' he replied,
'But I've no means of payment.'
'Not a problem,' soothed the girl,
'I'll take as pledge your raiment.

'Give me your belt, your seals and staff,
Deposit for a kid from your flock.'
Judah agreed and lay with her,
Defiling his own stock.

She slipped back to her home, removed her veil
And restored her widow's weeds;
Not knowing that within her womb
Were growing Judah's seeds.

Judah sent back, by the hand of a friend,
A kid for the prostitute;
But the townsmen affirmed that in their town
Were no women of ill-repute.

Three months on, and Judah was told
That Tamar was carrying a child,
Clearly conceived through harlotry –
A report that sent him wild!

'A wife in waiting! A heinous crime
Against our family and God!
Take her out and let her be burnt' –
A sentence confirmed on the nod.

Before being led to her execution,
She sent a package to Judah's home,
Bearing the message, 'Let my retribution
Be considered by you alone.
For that which grows within my womb
Was planted by the owner of these!' –
And from the package Judah removed
His belt, his staff and his seals!

He immediately stopped the execution,
Crying, 'Right is on her side!
For I disregarded her deepest emotion,
When a husband to her I denied.'

Six months later she was delivered of twins,
Perez and Zerach, in turn,
'Recompense for the two husbands I lost;
This I proudly affirm.'

# Joseph in Egypt
## (39:1–23)

The high ranking Potiphar,
Chief Steward of Pharaoh's court,
For delicate diplomatic tasks
Invariably sought
Out Joseph to execute them with style,
And never with so much as a tincture of guile.

Every problem Joseph could solve,
And was never deflected from his resolve.
Those whose dreams defied decoding,
He related directly to events unfolding.

Joseph's beauty was the talk of the court;
To capture his attention, women fought.
Men of rank sought his advice –
For which Potiphar extracted a considerable price! –
They all forgot he was but a slave,
He seemed so confident, wise and brave.
He had the demeanour of a prince
And his master acknowledged that ever since
He entered his service he'd been blessed
With prosperity and sweet success.

'It's the Hebrew God,' Said Potiphar,
'Who's placed him beneath his brightest star.'
But Joseph was soon to be sorely tested,
When his master's wife overtly invested
Much of her time and attention
On that lad, the new sensation.

Her husband was away so much of late,
That Joseph had to run the entire estate.
She leered at his beauty and his shoulder-length hair,
His graceful gait and incomparable flair.

'Lie with me,' one day she pleaded.
'No,' Said Joseph, 'If I acceded,
I would sin against God, as well as my master,
And that would be a double disaster!'

Day after day, she persisted,
Day after day, Joseph resisted.
One holiday, with her home deserted,
She did more than plead; she more than flirted.
She seized Joseph to satisfy her craving,
'Lie with me!' repeatedly raving.

So strong was her passion
And the embrace of her arms,
That Joseph almost gave in
To the lure of her charms!
Just then he recalled his aged father's face,
Neither smiling nor alight with its customary grace,
But pale and incensed, and covered in shame,
While pointing at Joseph a finger of blame.

'No, no,' cried Joseph, 'Am I insane?
There's no doubt that this can only end in pain.'
He broke loose with a mighty heave,
But she just managed to hold on to his sleeve.
Pulling off his cape in the melee –
While Joseph fled into the light of day.

A woman scorned is a dangerous foe,
But she was astute enough to know
That, given her flighty reputation,
They'd believe him, in spite of her station.

Immediately, she hatched a plan:
Tearing her blouse, she quickly ran
Outside, screaming, 'Help me, please!
That Hebrew lad would not release
Me until I agreed to submit to his will,
So I struggled and clawed and screamed until
A passer-by raised the alarm;
Then he tried to escape to avoid much harm,
But when, to restrain him, I grabbed hold of his cape,
He just slipped out of it and made good his escape.
And here it is for all to see –
The evidence to vindicate me!'

When Potiphar returned and heard her account
Of what had occurred with no one about,
He was understandably angry and started to shout,
Though his anger was tempered by considerable doubt,
For he'd observed his wife, on occasions past,
Flaunting herself before the last
Ambassador to Edom
When he returned to court –
While the attention of others she also sought.

How well he knew that tongues were wagging
At the many conquests of which she was bragging –
In confidence to her intimate friends,
Who whispered it around for their own ends!

Something was also quite mystifying,
Suggestive of the fact that his wife was lying!
She'd said she'd clawed in an attempt to resist –
But Joseph was unmarked on both face and wrist!

Potiphar sensed that his wife's allegation,
Her contradictory protestation
And more than sullied reputation,
Would make her the butt
Of the entire nation.

So, after a brief consideration,
He sentenced Joseph to incarceration
In the jail where ministers of the crown
Who'd offended Pharaoh were all sent down.

Even there, God kept his promise,
And appointed Joseph to a high office,
Directing every operation
From health and safety to administration,
Even to researching the legislation,
And attending to those on probation.

Never had a youth of twenty eight,
Let alone a Hebrew and an inmate –
Could one envisage a lowlier state? –
Been appointed to a prison directorate!

# The Butler and the Baker
(40:1–23)

Pharaoh's butler and baker got drunk one day,
And offended the king in a terrible way;
In Pharaoh's cup a fly was discovered,
While his bread, in wagon oil was smothered.
They were both assigned to Joseph's jail,
Pending any consideration of bail;
And while there, they each took to dreaming –
A repeated dream with no obvious meaning.

Joseph, seeing them so distraught,
Disclosed that his God had long ago taught
Him how to interpret a dream's import,
And that, if his special skill they sought,
It was free to them –
Not to be bought.

The butler related in detail his dream:
A three-branched vine he'd vividly seen,
Which budded, blossomed and ripened to grapes,
All in a moment –
Emergent shapes.

He squeezed them tightly with his hand,
Watched the red liquid gently land
Inside the royal goblet of solid gold –
Then presented it for Pharaoh to hold.

Without a moment's hesitation,
Joseph provided the elucidation:
'Whereas you beheld a three-branched vine,
This tells you that, in three days' time,
Pharaoh will restore you to your post,
Providing wine for his every toast.'

Joseph concluded by asking a favour:
'Sir, when your high rank again you savour,
Please mention my fate to the king,
For I am innocent of everything
That has been alleged by Potiphar's wife –
I was kidnapped from Canaan and the simple life.
I've never sinned in the manner described,
And the case against me was clearly contrived.

The king's baker rejoiced for his friend,
And prayed for himself such a happy end:
'A three-layered tray was in my dream,
The top one laden with loaves, cakes and cream;
I was carrying the tray on top of my head
When a bird came and ate
All the cakes and the bread!'

'Oh dear,' said Joseph, 'this is what it says:
The three-layered tray denotes three days,
After which you'll be hanged on a tree till you're dead,
And the birds of prey will peck at your head!'

Three days on, at his birthday celebration,
Pharaoh gave the servants their confirmation:
The butler, again, handed Pharaoh his cup;
As for the poor baker –
His time was up!

But the butler betrayed ingratitude,
And for two years did not allude
To the fate of Joseph, so unfairly condemned –
Till God brought his woes to an abrupt end.

## *Pharaoh's Dreams*
(41:1–36)

It was now Pharaoh's turn to dream –
For monarchs aren't as immune as they seem
To worrying about what the future might bring,
And whether they and their subjects
Will weep or sing.

He was standing by the Nile, where the reeds grow dense,
When he beheld a sight that made no sense:
From the reed grass seven cows stepped out,
Well-fed and sturdy, handsome and stout.

Before long, there followed the sound of feet,
Seven more cows, each pale as a sheet;
Ugly and gaunt, thin as a rake,
They approached the fat cows and proceeded to take
Them into their mouths and swallow them down –
At which Pharaoh awoke,
On his forehead a frown.

After tossing and turning, he fell back to sleep,
But, sadly for him, this didn't keep
Him from having a dream, much the same –
Not of cows this time,
But of stalks of grain.

Seven ears of corn, healthy and strong,
Grew on a single stalk;
Behind which sprouted seven thin ears,
The east wind had dried like chalk.

The withered ears then swallowed up
Their neighbours, fresh and full –
At which point Pharaoh awoke again,
Fearful in spirit and dull.

He called his magicians to elucidate,
But most were mystified;
When they started to concoct scenarios,
Pharaoh knew that they had lied.

'If, by tomorrow, I don't have the truth,'
He sternly told his court,
'Heads will roll from the palace roof –
I won't be sold short!'

That was enough to frighten
The butler out of his wits:
'Your majesty, I now recall
An interpreter who sits
In your own royal jail suffering
A truly sorry fate,
A Hebrew youth, once employed
On Potiphar's estate.

'He was together in the jail
With the baker and myself,
When we were both condemned for
Endangering the king's health.

'On the same night we both had dreams,
Comprising the most bizarre themes;
When that lad revealed just what they meant,
It left him dejected, but me content.

'The baker's most alarming dream,
Of birds picking at bread,
He explained accurately to mean
That he'd shortly lose his head.
And as for my squeezing of grapes
Into Pharaoh's cup –
He said that it betokened
The restoration of my luck.'

'Hurry,' said Pharaoh, 'bring me that lad.
Don't worry if his appearance looks bad.
Just wash him well and change his shirt,
For no disaster can I avert,
And with no foe can I contend,
Unless I know what the gods intend.'

Pharaoh told his dream to the Hebrew slave,
Who stood before him, surprisingly brave,
His spirits making a sudden revival,
With this chance to secure his own survival.

'Your majesty's dreams of cows and grain –
Both of them have the identical aim:
The Hebrew God, who guides my fate,
Is offering a life-line to the Egyptian state.

'The seven fat cows and ears of corn,
Are seven years that are about to dawn,
With Egypt blessed with an abundance of food,
Putting it into a euphoric mood.

'But just as the lean ones followed in tow,
And devoured the fat – though no one would know –
So, seven lean years will then arrive,
Bringing such starvation that few will survive.

'The double dream was God's revelation,
Intended to convey his determination
To bring about swiftly this situation –
But to convey as well its alleviation.'

'What do you mean, lad, by "alleviation?" '
Interrupted Pharaoh, with agitation.
Your words strike me as prevarication,
For how can we thwart God's premeditation?'

'Your Majesty, my words are true;
For God has given me the very clearest view
Of how to avoid this catastrophe,
Through storage of grain and a tax levy.'

'Speak on, sir, you have my ear,'
Urged Pharaoh, bringing Joseph near.
'The plan, Sir, needs an overseer,
An agronomist whose way is clear
To build storage plants throughout the land,
For corn levied
By royal command.

'His men will assess fields nationwide,
And seize a fifth to be put aside
During the seven years when stocks abound,
So, when famine stalks,
Food may be found.'

## Joseph's rise to power
### (41:37–57)

Pharaoh's courtiers looked in dismay
At Joseph who'd offered an ingenious way
To avoid the looming devastation,
And convert it into sweet salvation.

'I've never beheld one so wise,'
Exclaimed Pharaoh with surprise,
'In whom God's spirit so resides –
A veritable seer in a slave's disguise.

'I hereby place you in total charge,
Not just for this project of State,
For I shall entrust to your hands
The country's entire fate.

'Your commands shall be obeyed
As if they were my own;
Above you there is but one rank,
And that's the royal throne.'

Pharaoh thereupon invested Joseph
With robes, signet and chain,
And addressed him as Zafnat Paneah,
To replace his Hebrew name.

He gave him Asenat, an Egyptian wife,
Daughter of the Priest of On,
Assigning to him a royal chariot
And a most impressive home.

Heralds ran ahead of him,
Commanding all, *Abrek!* –
"Attention! The ruler comes!
Let everyone bend their neck!"

Joseph was but thirty
When he attained this high rank;
But, recalling his youthful dreams,
He knew he'd God to thank.

The seven years of plenty came,
Just as foretold;
And much of each year's harvest
Was stored, rather than sold.

During that time, Asenat
Bore Joseph two boys,
Named Menasseh and Ephraim,
To express his new-found joys:
Menasseh – "God made me forget" –
All my youthful woes;
Ephraim – "He made me prosper"
In the land of my sorrows.

The seven years of famine
Really began to bite.
No swelling Nile in Summer months –
An eagerly awaited sight –
The result of torrential rain
In the basin of the upper Nile,
Flowing to the Delta below,
To render it fertile.
But now those parts were arid,
No water was carried down;
And the fields that once were moist and green,
Were now all yellowy brown.

All the citizens of Egypt
Came starving to the king.
'Speak to Joseph,' he replied,
'I've given him my ring!'

Joseph opened the granaries
Throughout Egypt's land;
Even serving out the rations
With his own royal hand.

All the surrounding countries
Suffered the same fate;
Children staring blankly
At their empty plate.

They all turned to Egypt
For help in their plight;
And hence it was that Jacob
Had that country in his sight.

# Reunion of Joseph and his Brothers
## (42:1–11)

Joseph knew it was but a matter of time –
For the situation in Canaan was far from fine –
Before his brothers would come and bow
Before his royal presence, precisely how
He'd dreamed it all those years before –
Though with no intimation of an Egyptian store –
With sheaves emerging and bending the knee,
Fully confirming the divine decree.

To his guards he issued the clear order,
To note each arrival at the border;
And, on each hour of every day,
To relay that information without delay.
He closed every distribution centre,
Save the one through which all had to enter.

'Go down to Egypt and buy some grain,'
Said Jacob, 'but, to prevent more pain,
I'll not send Benjamin as he's only a lad,
And mustn't suffer, like Joseph, anything bad.'

The brothers travelled to Egypt,
To Joseph's distribution bay,
Where they bowed down twice to the ground
Before attempting to pay.

Joseph naturally recognised them
As soon as they appeared;
His own face was now transformed
By the addition of a beard.

Joseph's emotions were taut and confused;
Should he now take revenge for how they'd abused
And thrown him into that deep, dark pit,
Where he'd been unable to stand or sit?

But if he did so, what would he gain?
It would be his father who'd suffer most pain.
He could well be starving at this very time,
Awaiting his sons,
Bearing oil, corn and wine.

Or maybe his dad was long since dead?
That thought filled him with the utmost dread;
How could he extract that information
Without betraying that he was a relation?

He was also desperate to discover
If they regretted their treatment of their brother;
As well as needing a master plan,
To bring down to Egypt
The entire clan.

## Allegation of Espionage!
### (42:12–17)

In a flash, it all fell into place;
And, setting aside his customary grace,
He charged them brusquely with being spies,
Saying, he would assuredly brook no lies.
'You are clearly ten scouts of the Canaanite forces,
Come to assess our military resources!'

'No Viceroy,' they all cried together.
'We are simple shepherds, we have never
Been enlisted into any troop;
It's our father who sent us as a group,
To bring back food because we were starving –
As were the cattle that we were farming.'

'Tell me more,' barked Joseph, 'let me hear
About this father whom you hold so dear,
And any more brothers who, as we speak,
May be ferreting out where Egypt is weak!'

'No, Viceroy, you misconstrue
The sole objective we have in view.
Our father, Jacob, is an elderly man,
Venerable head of an expanding clan.
Twelve sons he begat – one, alas, was lost;
Family grief still stalks us, to our cost.
For every minute of every day,
The feeling of loss won't go away!'

Joseph swallowed the lump in his throat –
Pretending to straighten the hem of his coat –
'Did he die of an ailment or a marauder's sword?'
He asked nonchalantly, as he poured
A glass of wine to wet his parched lips –
Scrutinising each face between his sips.

'Sir,' said Simeon, 'we know not his fate.
Some traders seized him – that's all we can state.
'Oh, how we wish we'd displayed more care –
The boy's loss is our family's nightmare.'

Joseph paused for a moment or two –
His questions answered exactly on cue.
Simeon added: 'Only Benjamin is left,
Whom father kept back fearing he'd be bereft
Of him as he was of his older brother,
Joseph, whom he loved more than any other.'

'Did that special love bother you at all?'
'It did, Viceroy, as we recall.
But that is now so long in the past,
And jealousy shouldn't be allowed to last!'

Joseph's eyes were now moist with tears.
Had they truly repented over the years?
But he had to enable his plan to run,
If sun, moon and stars were ever to come
And bow down to him as his dreams had foretold –
Those dreams that had led to him being sold.

'Prove to me that you are not spies,
By verifying your family ties.
That Benjamin, to whom you referred –
Who, on his own now tends the herd –
I wish to see him with my own eyes,
To satisfy myself
That you are not spies.'

# A Ruse to bring Benjamin to Egypt
## (42:18–43:16)

Three days later their permits came through.
To receive their grain they stood in the queue,
Before Joseph, who had more to say:
'Your brother, Simeon, will have to stay
Behind in Egypt while you all return
And persuade your father – be gentle but firm! –
To allow Benjamin to leave his side;
For, if he does not, Simeon will be tried,
Sentenced and punished with decapitation
As befits a spy for a foreign nation.'

The brothers fell into each other's arms,
Petitioning God with cries and psalms.
'We're being punished for drowning out
Our brother Joseph's anguished shout.'

They expressed their fear in the Hebrew tongue,
So the Viceroy would not understand;
Once again, Joseph had to withdraw
To an anteroom close at hand.

He commanded his aide to fill up their sacks
With the grain they had all sought,
But to place in each sack the silver coins
They'd produced when they had bought.

They stopped at an inn to spend the night,
But their asses first had to be fed.
They opened their sacks, and at the sight
Of their money their hearts turned to lead.

They arrived back home and told their dad
All that had occurred.
'God of my fathers,' he wailed, 'that's bad;
Has anyone ever heard
Of a single family with so many woes,
Of children almost coming to blows,
Of a precious son a wild beast's prey,
Of corn provided without having to pay,
Of another son being cast into jail
To prove they all hadn't concocted a tale
To camouflage their evil intent –
That on espionage they were really bent?
'How can I allow Benjamin to leave
When, for Joseph, I've still not ceased to grieve?
He links my soul to Rachel, his mother,
And keeps fresh the memory of his older brother!'

A few months passed, and there was no more grain,
So Jacob requested his children again
To return to Egypt to buy some more
From the Viceroy,
With his limitless store.

'Father,' the brothers impatiently cried:
'To prove to the man that we've not lied,
We must present Benjamin for him to behold,
Either that, or Simeon – as you've been told –
Will lose his head in that Egyptian jail,
And our plea for food will not avail.'

Jacob simply had to concede,
Especially when Judah guaranteed
To bring back safe young Benjamin –
Or forfeit the lives of his next of kin.

Before they left, Jacob gave advice
That they take to the Viceroy some choicest spice,
Honey and almonds and delicacies rare,
Canaanite figurines – a matching pair –
And return the money that, behind their backs,
Had been replaced maliciously in their sacks.

## Further trials for the brothers
(43:17–44:34)

When they arrived back for their fateful meeting,
Joseph's steward offered a curious greeting:
'Don't worry. The money returned to you all
Was a gift from your God in response to your call.
For we've received payment for the grain supplied –
And, if this is Benjamin, then you've clearly not lied,
And we've no further reason
To keep Simeon inside.'

When Joseph returned to his home and found
His brothers there, prostrate to the ground,
He expressed his thanks for the gifts received,
Asked about their father, and was much relieved
When they said he was alive and well,
So that, as far as Joseph could now tell,
He had time on his hands to bring down
To Egypt his father, his glory, his crown.

It was then that he noticed Benjamin,
Standing meekly by Judah's side;
He went over and blessed him,
That he might ever be God's pride.

He then proceeded to invite them all
To join him for a meal at table.
He seated them in order of age –
They were astounded how he was able!

To each brother he presented one gift,
To reciprocate what they'd brought;
But to Benjamin, his own mother's son,
Five rings, exquisitely wrought.

This was a test to determine
If envy still lurked in their breast;
But would they abandon Benjamin
At a Viceroy's behest?

To ascertain this, he told his steward
To fill their sacks to the top,
And into young Benjamin's,
Joseph's silver cup to drop.

Now this was no ordinary cup
From which Joseph sipped;
With this he pretended to divine
The future for Egypt.

The brothers left, their spirits high,
Putting behind them the question why
They'd been made to suffer tribulation
At the hands of the head of the Egyptian nation.

Before very long, Joseph sent an aide
To overtake the brothers and severely upbraid
Them for such an unpardonable act of theft
From the Viceroy, Joseph, before they left.

They couldn't believe what was being alleged;
So resolute they were in denial,
That death to the thief they immediately pledged
And jail for the rest without trial.

A search was conducted of every sack –
So thoroughly it took the brothers aback –
And when the cup was found with Benjamin's corn,
They all screamed and rued the day they were born.

They rent their clothes; were brought back to the city,
Disconsolate and wallowing in pity
For the plight of their brother –
More than for their own –
And for their father who was now
So completely alone.

Joseph was waiting with a regal air
When the brothers entered in total despair:
'What shall we say? What shall we declare?
The Lord, our sin, has this day laid bare.'

'We're all your servants,' said Judah in sorrow.
'Far be it!' said Joseph, 'You'll return home tomorrow!
I'll keep here just the one who stole,
The rest of you have an old dad to console!'

At that, Judah just lost control:
'You know full well that the lad never stole.
There's clearly some intrigue afoot,
Though I'm currently unable to put
My finger on what it might be about,
But I'll find out the truth –
I have no doubt.
You don't frighten me, Viceroy, with your upper hand –
Neither does Pharaoh, king of your land;
For unless we all return, safe and sound,
You'll suffer reprisals from our allies around.

'We've been nothing but honest since we first arrived;
Though, to get Benjamin here, you've clearly connived,
Inflicting on us some fearful tricks,
Employing some most unworthy tactics.

'I swore an oath to our aged dad,
That I'd bring back safely his beloved lad.
A doubly-broken heart he can't survive,
So Benjamin must return alive.

'Our father communes with God above,
Who guaranteed him safety as well as love;
So, know, Viceroy, with whom you trifle,
For the consequence will be truly frightful.
Rather than send him to an early grave,
Release the lad and take me as your slave.'

At the sound of those words, Joseph choked –
His own situation they acutely evoked.
How far the brothers had come since that day;
How much they'd changed,
They could no more betray!

## *Joseph discloses his identity*
### (45:1–28)

Tears, again, rolled down his face;
His heart was stirred as he longed to embrace
His brothers, and disclose to them
Who it was that chose to condemn
As spies such patently innocent men.

So he demanded that all his servants leave
His presence immediately;
He then proceeded to reveal
His real identity.

'I am Joseph' –
The brothers turned cold! –
'I'm your brother whom you sold.
Approach and let me embrace you all,
And in my arms enfold.

'It was God's design that you carried out,
Not just your own will;
I had to be sold to preserve many lives –
A bitter-sweet pill!

'I also feel the need to explain
How deeply I felt the pain
Of inflicting on you such terrible things,
Taking advantage of the power of kings.

'But I had to be sure that you'd learnt from the past,
And would never view a brother as an outcast;
And the dreams of my youth had to be fulfilled
Exactly as the good Lord willed.

'Now, hurry home and bring dad down;
I've reserved for you an Egyptian town
In Goshen, the district where you'll live,
And prosper through initiative.
Pharaoh welcomes your presence here –
To his laws ever be sure to adhere –
Twenty wagons laden with grain
He'll send with other foods to sustain
You until your families all come down –
When you'll have an audience with the crown.'

— ✦✦ —

# Jacob and family settle in Egypt
## (46:1–7, 28–47:27)

Seventy of Jacob's offspring
Made the journey down,
And word spread through Egypt
That a man of great renown –
The father of their Viceroy –
Shortly would alight;
So they gathered in their thousands,
To express their delight.

Joseph was the first
To greet his aged dad;
One dressed in royal robes,
The other as a shepherd clad.

They fell around each other's neck,
Tears fusing cheek to cheek.
They had so many things to say,
But neither of them could speak.

At last, Jacob, finding his voice,
Looked into his son's eyes:
'Now I can die having seen your face,
Farewell my sorrows and sighs.'

Joseph proceeded to prime his brothers
For their audience with Pharaoh the king:
'Say you are owners of vast herds –
The impression is everything!'

But the brothers were all simple folk,
Not given to exaggeration:
'We tend sheep,' they told Pharaoh –
To Joseph's consternation!

When He was presented to the king,
Jacob blessed him to his face:
'May the One who grants thee royal estate
Forever show thee grace.'

'How old are you, my venerable man?'
Pharaoh asked his guest.
'One hundred and thirty years, royal sir,
All marked by joys suppressed.'

Pharaoh was drawn to the man,
And the light he radiated;
His life of pain, of loss and grief
Was nowhere indicated.

'Your sons, I hear, are herdsmen skilled.
Now Joseph's plan, as you know, is to build
Vast pens to enclose the flocks we'll take
From all my subjects in the wake
Of the crippling famine that's about to arrive,
Making it impossible to survive
Without exchanging cattle – every head,
For what we've stored of corn for bread.

'This is where your sons fit in;
They'll be the lynch-pin,
Of the entire administration
Of what we acquire by sequestration:
From the health and welfare of each flock
To the breeding of new live-stock.
And if they meet with success,
To untold wealth they'll gain access.

'You are most welcome in my land;
To all your family I extend the hand
Of friendship and co-operation –
Hail, new nobility
Of the Egyptian nation!'

Joseph's plan was executed:
The land of Egypt was state-looted,
As the deeds of every field
Were handed in for their yield
Of state-supplied and packaged grain –
A life-line when there was no rain.

The dispossessed population
Had to suffer relocation;
Some in cities incarcerated –
Hatred of Hebrews openly stated.

Others became tenant farmers,
Paying a fifth in rent from their garners;
Only the priests were saved that fate;
No compulsory purchase of their estate.

The Israelites soon put down roots,
Enjoying newly-embraced pursuits;
They prospered greatly and multiplied,
Their influence felt country-wide.

# Jacob's last days
## (47:28–48:22)

For seventeen years Jacob enjoyed
His life in Egypt, spirits buoyed
By Joseph's position and his sons' success –
Though Joseph visited less and less.

He assumed it was his son's engagements,
And the security arrangements,
As Joseph's popularity was alarmingly low,
With citizens' prosperity now at zero.

But Joseph had to pay another visit,
Because news reached him that his father's spirit
Was much depressed through shortness of breath;
And his family feared he was close to death.

Joseph rushed to his father's bedside,
With his two sons, his joy and pride.
'Who are these?' wheezed Jacob, nonplussed,
Joseph gulped –
'Have we never discussed
Ephraim and Menasseh, my Egyptian Hebrews?
Have I never shared with you their news?'

'Don't worry, son;
You'd other things on your mind.
But now's the time – if you'll be so kind –
To promise to fulfil my last request:
Don't bury me here, but in the land that's blessed
By our father in heaven seven-fold,
In the cave of Machpelah –
Our ancestral foothold.'

'Your wish, father, is my command;
I'll take your remains myself to that land.
But, for now, consider the next generation –
Make my sons leaders of the Israelite nation.'

'I will, my son, if that's their desire,
If to that position they aspire;
Let there be not one Joseph tribe,
But Ephraim and Menasseh
As two I'll inscribe.'

Joseph brought them to his father's side,
Placing Menasseh, the firstborn, at his right with pride;
But Jacob crossed his right hand to Ephraim's head,
Bestowing on him the main blessing, instead:

'*God make you like Ephraim and Menasseh,*
Joseph's fine offspring.'
With these words, for their children,
Men will invoke blessing.

# Jacob's deathbed blessing
## (49:1-32)

Jacob called in all his sons:
'I'll now reveal how the future runs;
For the good Lord has invested me –
Albeit to a small degree –
With prophetic ability.

'To you, Reuben, what can I say?
Your sin was great when you lay
With Bilhah – to your father's shame –
For which you'll forfeit
The firstborn's claim.

'Simeon and Levi –
I lump you together –
Wherever you are
There's stormy weather.
Cursed be your anger
And your retribution;
Be scattered in Israel
Suffer substitution.

'Judah is a lion's whelp,
Fearless and astute;
Head of the tribal pack,
Receiving its tribute.
In physique strong and imposing,
Eyes sparkling like red wine;
Teeth whiter than the whitest milk,
Set in a strong jaw-line.

'The ruler's staff, from your stock,
Never shall depart;
Their foes' most violent machinations
They'll skilfully outsmart.
This will last until the time
When to Shiloh men will flow,
At that time their full allegiance
On God will they bestow.

'Zebulun's tribe, I foresee,
By Canaan's coast-line dwelling,
As far as Tyre, in the north –
In maritime trade excelling.

'Issachar will use all his strength
To do menial work and farm;
Preferring to pay invaders' tribute,
Than militarily arm.

'From Dan shall come the judges,
Sifting evidence with care;
Pouncing, like a serpent,
When falsehood is laid bare.

'Gad will need a standing army
To keep enemies in his sight;
To repel his most warlike neighbours –
Aramaean and Moabite.

'Asher's name, "contentment,"
Will reflect his state of mind;
A bread-basket his land shall be –
Delicacies of every kind.

'Naphtali's eloquence of speech
Pours forth like a hind in flight;
May he inspire generations
To look for spiritual light.

'Joseph is a fruitful vine
Whose branches just keep growing;
May his guidance and his counsel
Keep perennially flowing.

'There were those among you
Who dealt him bitter blows;
But his faith, like armour,
Resisted your arrows.

'May the Lord, my Protector,
Of his blessings, bestow
On you and your family
The choicest things that grow;
May you become prolific
Dandling babes on your knee,
And may the happiness you enjoy
Exceed that vouchsafed to me.

'Benjamin, my youngest son,
With much you've had to cope;
But that has toughened you so much
That men will only hope
That you will be on their side,
Not an adversary;
For when aroused, you're like a wolf,
Tearing prey most violently.'

Jacob then blessed each of them,
Repeating his final request,
That they take his remains to Machpelah,
In the land that he loved best.

## Death and burial of Jacob
### (49: 33–50:14)

Jacob then gave up his soul,
Ending his troubled earthly role.
Joseph fell on his neck and wept,
Finding it difficult to accept
The brevity of time he'd spent with his dad,
Just the seventeen years when he was a lad.

A conscience pang then set in:
All father's pain had been caused by him!
The brotherly strife that nearly got him killed,
His selfish dreams that had to be fulfilled,
Causing an aged dad to come and bow down
To settle in an alien country and town.
How he must have pined each day
For a visit from the son who'd stayed away,
And whose state duties just seemed to weigh
More importantly than to display
Some love until dad's dying day.

A public mourning was declared,
For seventy days was the body prepared
By those licensed to embalm –
While Joseph led prayer and choral psalm.

Pharaoh permitted the journey to be made,
His treasury covering all the bills to be paid.
He dispatched his own charioteers,
With some officials shedding tears.

They buried Jacob in the hallowed ground,
And eulogised his most profound
Influence on all around,
As father, seer, and man renowned,
Who mourned for a son then saw him crowned;
Who took the sting out of a brother's hurt,
Leaving him content with his own desert;
Who won the respect of the Egyptian throne,
Though maimed by an angel on his thigh bone.

After seven days of mourning
They all turned around,
And journeyed back to Egypt
Without any sound;
Wrapped in thought about the departed,
And all the values he'd imparted.

## The brothers' apprehension
(50: 15-21)

But the brothers' minds were now distracted,
By the distant manner in which Joseph had acted
Towards them even at the interment –
What if there'd been but a deferment,
Of Joseph's plan for retribution,
And after father's death –
Execution?

So an intercessor was sent to speak
To Joseph, earnestly to seek
Forgiveness for all they'd perpetrated
In those far off days
When he'd been hated.
He reported that their father's last wish
Had been that Joseph should not punish
His brothers at all for their boyish
Jealousy and his anguish,
But accept their plea and forgive their sin,
Granting clemency to them and their kin.

The brothers then entered and fell on the ground,
Uttering a deep-throated, wailing sound:
'We'll be your slaves, but spare our lives;
Inflict no pain on our children and wives.'

Joseph burst into a flood of tears,
And couldn't believe that over all those years
Suspicion had lurked in his dad's heart
That his desire for revenge might never depart.

'Why is it?' – He asked himself aloud –
'That, unlike father, I was not endowed
With the ability to make, of a foe, a friend,
And bring strained relations to a speedy end?

'My brothers,' he retorted, 'be not afraid;
Let all your fears be allayed.
I may conceal the love I feel,
But I'm truly pained now at your ordeal.
I do forgive you, with all my heart,
And pray that this will indeed be the start
Of a new bond that we'll all enjoy –
Forget my status as Viceroy –
To protect you all shall be my goal,
For that was, truly, my heaven-sent role.'

## *Joseph's final farewell*
### (50: 22–26)

Joseph lived to a hundred and ten,
A great, great grandpa he was when
He felt his days approaching their end,
And begged his offspring to attend
To his final wish that, when they returned
To the Promised Land for which they'd yearned,
They should take his remains there,
To be interred.

They readily complied with Joseph's request,
And, once embalmed, he was placed in a chest
Within a temple especially blessed
To await his eternal rest
In the land that Jacob's offspring possessed.

# END

# NOTES TO THE TEXT
## Sources of Inspiration

In our Introduction we have referred to the great indebtedness of this work to the rabbinic literature of Talmud and Midrash, as well as to Judaism's medieval and modern commentaries. The Midrash Bereshit Rabba – a distillation of rabbinic expositions on the book of Genesis – was the source which triggered most of my creative ideas. In the notes that follow, I identify those sources and explain my purpose in situations where I have diverted from their literal implication or used them 'creatively.'

A poem is also a commentary; and not a few of my own insights, fruits of a lifetime of biblical research and publication (see **www.rabbijeffrey. co.uk**), are also embedded within the text. For this reason, as well as to clarify the latter, I decided to accompany the poem with these background notes. Apart from their intrinsic interest, educationalists or students of Bible might well find them useful as an educational tool. It might be instructive to compare our poetic version with the biblical text. As it is much easier to read the poem than the English translations, the former might be read first, by way of introduction to the biblical narrative.

The rich, imaginative and spiritually arousing comments of the Midrash are well worthy of study and analysis; and a further objective of these notes is to introduce the student or general reader to that particular genre of Jewish Bible commentary. If read in a classroom or study circle, the teacher might wish to deal more fully with the sources I employ.

The supreme master of the medieval school of rabbinic commentary was Rabbi Shlomo Yitzchaki (1040–1105), popularly referred to by the acronym of his name, *Rashi*. With the arrival of printing (15th cent.), his commentary was accorded prominence in every edition of the Hebrew Bible, and, not surprisingly, I have relied greatly on his work.

It is to be hoped that these notes – like the poetry itself – will excite the imagination of the reader by exposing him or her to an abundance of new insights and issues for consideration, thus inspiring them to further and deeper biblical study. Perhaps such an exercise will also explain how it is that Judaism's ancient biblical and rabbinic literature continues to attract more and more students to immerse themselves in its study each year at seminaries, especially in Israel, and why an increasing number of laymen and women are thronging adult education programmes throughout the Jewish world.

★ ★ ★

## References and abbreviations

The left-hand references are to page and stanza numbers of the poetry. Thus, 28:4 denotes page 28, stanza 4.

To avoid confusion, references to chapters and verses in Genesis are prefaced by the abbreviation 'Gen.,' such as Gen. 32:1. Where a simple reference, such as 32:1, occurs, this refers to the page and stanza of the poetry.

Each chapter of Midrash is divided into sub sections. Thus 8 [5] refers to chapter 8, section 5 of the standard editions.

The following abbreviations have been employed: Av. Zar., for (Talmud) Avodah Zarah; B.M., for (Talmud) Baba Metzi'a; Bem. Rabb., for (Midrash) Bemidbar Rabba; Ber. Rab., for (Midrash) Bereshit Rabba; Deut., for Deuteronomy; Eccl., for Ecclesiastes; Eiruv., for (Talmud) Eiruvin; Ex., for Exodus; Gen., for Genesis; Is., for Isaiah; Jer., for Jeremiah; Lev., for Leviticus; Mid., for Midrash; Mid. Tanch., for Midrash Tanchuma; n. for note; Nid., for (Talmud) Niddah; p. for page; Ps. for psalm; R., for Rabbi; Rab., for Rabba; San. for (Talmud) Sanhedrin; Shabb., for (Talmud) Shabbat; Tal. for Talmud; v., for verse; vv., for verses.

## Notes

### Creation

1:2 *Those who would morally cower:* This sentiment echoes the psalmist's exclamation, 'Lord, what is man that you (desire to) know him, or the son of man that you even consider him' (Ps.144:3–4). These verses, which constitute a most appropriate introduction to the Memorial Prayers for the Departed, recited in synagogues on festivals, draw attention to the problem of how weak and sinful man can possibly justify his own creation and his Maker's concern, indulgence and forgiveness. The opening stanzas of the poem address this problem, with the heavenly beings cast in the role of accusers, questioning God as to the logic of his purpose.

1:3 *The angels of the heavenly host:* 'R. Simon said: When God came to create Adam, the ministering angels were divided into various factions, some saying, "let him be created," and others saying "let him not be created." This is the sense of the verse: *Kindness and truth meet; righteousness and peace kiss* (Ps. 85:1). Kindness said, "Let him be created, for he will dispense kindness;" truth said: "Let him not be created, for he is essentially false." Righteousness said: "Let him be created, for he will perform deeds of righteousness;" peace said, "Let him not be created, for he is naturally inclined to strife" (Ber. Rab. 1[8]).

2:1 *A cheery cherub:* 'Cherub' is a translation of the biblical Hebrew word *keruv*. This refers to a category of angels that are supposed to surround the divine chariot, as referred to in the famous vision of Ezekiel (10:14). They appear for the first time in Gen. 3:24, as angelic beings, armed with flaming swords, and charged with barring the way of Adam's re-entry into the Garden of Eden. A less threatening, though similarly protective mission was fulfilled by the two golden cherubim, with out-stretched wings, that sat atop the Ark in Israel's desert sanctuary (see Ex. 25:20). Later Jewish tradition had it that those latter cherubim had the faces of a little boy and girl, respectively. It was probably that association which invested the term 'cherub' with its connotation of child-like innocence. It is with this connotation that I employ the notion of the 'cheery cherub' whose innocence enables him to chide God with impunity.

2:2 *Manifest fact:* 'R. Huna, Rabbi of Sepphoris, stated: While the ministering angels were busy, locked in debate over the issue, God went ahead and created Adam. God thereupon said to them: "What is the use of your discussion; man is now *manifest fact*" ' (Ber. Rab. 8 [5]).

2:4 *Let there be light!:* See Gen. 1:3.
  *A measured time for day and night:* See Gen. 1:3-5, 14-18.
  *Let rain descend from skies above:* Curiously, although Gen. 1:7 refers to God having created a space, or 'firmament,' to separate the waters above from those below, there is no mention in chapter 1 of clouds or of rain descending on the earth. It is only in chapter 2 that this matter is clarified. There we are told that after Creation was completed, but before the appearance of man, God 'caused a mist to ascend from the earth (dew?) to moisten its surface (Gen. 2:5-6). The Talmud explains that, although God had already created all the vegetation on the third day (Gen. 1:11-13), he kept it submerged beneath the surface of the earth until after the arrival of man. For that reason he did not cause rain to

fall at that time; and hence the absence of any reference to it. God's purpose in so delaying the rain – which caused the vegetation to spring forth – was so that man might discover for himself the necessity for rain, and pray accordingly for it to be sent to activate vegetation (Tal. Hullin 60b; Rashi on Gen. 2:5).

That vegetation was not, literally, 'brought forth' (v.12) on the third day is obvious from the fact that the sun, which is vital for the growth of vegetation, was not created until the fourth day! This consideration alone is proof that the Genesis account was never meant to constitute a scientific statement of the 'how' or precise chronology of Creation, but rather is to be understood as a poem of praise to its grandeur and awesome complexity, and to the Creator who designed its integrated components in order to facilitate human life and to provide a comforting and welcoming environment for it to flourish.

2:5 *Zigzag the space:* The image of rivers 'zigzaging' countries designated for human habitation is suggested by Gen. 2:10-14.

2:6 *Cool and cold and warmth and heat:* See Gen. 8:22.

3:2 *Seraph:* This term occurs in Deut. 8:15, as a description of a 'viper'. In the later biblical books it is the popular name for 'a fiery angel', on account of its root *s-r-ph*, 'to burn'. Hence, Isaiah's vision of 'a Seraph flying towards (him) with a burning coal in its hand' (6:6).

4:2 *Is that what you'd bless?:* The idea of man and the angels in perpetual contention on the issue of man's creation, with the latter ever eager to dissuade God from his purpose, reached its most explicit expression in the book of Job, where Satan wrests permission from God so that he may prove that even the faith of the most righteous among men, as exemplified by Job, can evaporate in the face of severe trial and tribulation. See Job 1:6-12.

*A world of darkness:* Darkness, in biblical literature, is a metaphor for moral chaos, as in the verse, 'The eyes of the wise man are in his head, but the fool walks in darkness (Eccl. 2:14). Isaiah viewed the mission of Israel as that of becoming 'a light to the nations, opening eyes that are blind, bringing forth the prisoner from his dungeon and those that dwell in darkness out of their constraints' (42:7). In the later literature of the Dead Sea Scrolls, the Essene writers referred to the final confrontation, at the end of time, between the forces of good and evil, as the war between 'The Sons of Light' and 'The Sons of Darkness.'

4:3 *"Regret" is a term of man's invention:* Although we have confined the concept of 'regret' to man, there is no denying that the Bible does employ the term in relation to God, as in the verse, 'And God said: I will destroy the man I have created from off the face of the earth...for I regret that I have made him (Gen.1:7. See also Gen. 6:7). The difference is that human regret follows the realization that the path previously trodden was wrong. God's regret is not based on any previous error of choice. For God, 'everything is foreseen' (Ethics of the Fathers 3:19). His 'regret' is simply that, in their exercise of the free choice bestowed by God, men frequently act in a misguided manner, contrary to His will, forcing Him to express his displeasure and impose punishment.

4:4 *I'm from the first until the last:* See Is. 44:6.

*I am its place:* This is based on the rabbinic concept of the relation of God to His world: 'The universe is not (the extent of) His place; He is the place of the universe' (Mid. *Pesikta Rabb.*, sec. 21). The first part of the quote refutes Spinoza's pantheistic identification of God with nature. The second part suggests that God's transcendence does not mean that he is detached from the world. In fact, His Spirit attaches itself to it with a kind of spiritual gravity.

5:1 *And stilled forever will be strife's sound:* This optimistic vision of the future is majestically expressed by Isaiah:

> Thus said the Lord, He that created the heavens and stretched them forth, He that spread forth the earth and that which issued from it; He that gives breath unto the people upon it and spirit to them that walk in it. I, the Lord, have called you in righteousness, and have taken hold of your hand, kept you and set you for a covenant of humanity, for a light to the nations (42:5-6).

## Adam

8:1 *There've been other worlds before this one:* This concept is inspired by the statement of R. Abbahu in the Midrash: 'God created worlds and destroyed them, created worlds and destroyed them, until he made ours. Then He said: "The previous worlds found no favour with me; this one does" (Ber. Rab.9 [2]).'

Many fundamentalist believers, who reject the scientific view of the antiquity of the world, and take literally the traditionalist view – rooted in Midrash – that it is only some 5,770 years, seek to explain away the remains of dinosaurs and other fossils by claiming that they are relics of those earlier worlds that God created and replaced. Some have suggested that the creation of the great sea-monsters (Gen. 1:21) also refers to those inhabitants of earlier worlds. The problem with such an identification is that the account in Genesis is of the creation of *our* world alone.

Rashi identifies those monsters with the great Leviathan and his mate. In order to prevent them procreating and inundating the world, God is credited with having slain the female and preserved her as food to be provided for the righteous in the World to Come (Mid. Ber. Rab. 7 [4]).

8:2 *"Shalom, brother":* Hebrew, *Shalom chaver!* This popular Modern Hebrew greeting became popularized when it was used, in November 1995, by the American President, Bill Clinton, in a eulogy to the assassinated Israeli Premier, Yitchak Rabin.

8:4 *Who, mysteriously, was making him wait:* While there is no biblical source for this particular episode, yet, on the verse, 'And God saw all that he had made, and behold it was very good (Gen.1:31), the Midrash states that, at that moment, God said to his world: "World, world, O that you would forever find such favour in my eyes as you do at this time" (Ber. Rab. 9 [4]). Adam's desperate wish to discern whether his offspring would live up to this challenge is clearly within the spirit of that Midrash.

In the same vein, another Midrash states that God showed Adam a vision of every future generation of leaders and sages (Ber. Rab. 24 [2]), perhaps with a view to reassuring him with regard to the merit of his offspring and the accumulated wisdom that might help them avoid sin and secure eternity.

9:2 *I will not move from my place:* In Judaism there is a long tradition of leaping to the defense of any condemned group or nation, whether deserving or otherwise, on even the slimmest chance of success. The first chronicled example is Abraham's spirited and courageous appeal against God's decision to destroy the wicked inhabitants of Sodom and Gomorrah.

We have credited Adam with having refused to move from his place until God reassures him that his offspring will merit divine grace and will never suffer destruction.

*Slipped into an induced sleep:* We have attempted here to bring out the full force of the biblical expression, 'And *God caused* a deep sleep to fall on Adam' (Gen. 3:21). Our version departs from the text by suggesting that Adam, through the exhaustion of crying out the whole night, simply fell into a deep sleep. We have employed the vague term 'induced sleep' in order to bridge the gap between the two versions of events found in Gen. 1:27 and 2:21–22, respectively.

## Eve

9:3 *Of being opened up and then sewn…* The biblical text states: 'And he took one of his ribs and built up the flesh in the place of it' (3:21). The Midrash suggests that God chose to create Eve from the rib on account of it being a concealed limb, symbolizing thereby the modesty that woman was expected to exhibit at all times (Ber. Rab. 18 [3]).

*No more alone* The Talmud contains an ethical gem, accounting for the fact that God created just one man at the outset, rather than immediately populating the earth:

> It comes to teach us that whoever destroys a single life is accountable as if (s)he had destroyed the entire world; and whoever saves a single life is considered to have saved the entire world. Another explanation is that it was in order to promote peace between people, so that no individual could say, "My ancestry is more noble than yours." It also testifies to the greatness of God, for, when a man mints many coins from a single seal, they are all identical; but God minted every human being from the seal of Adam, yet no two are wholly identical. Hence, every person is entitled to proclaim, "For my sake the world was created" (Tal. San. 38a).

The same Talmudic source then explains why God did not create every face identical. This was, 'so that no one, seeing a beautiful woman or house, could falsely assert, "that one is mine"'.

9:4 *Before him stood a vision unique:* The mystical book of Zohar (See on Sidrah Kedoshim) attributes it to Eve's overwhelming beauty that she and Adam only had children after they were banished from the Garden of Eden. Until then, Adam was unable to gaze at the lustre of her face. The sin reduced that beauty, enabling them to have a normal relationship.

The Midrash describes God as adorning Eve with twenty four ornaments before taking her by the hand and bringing her to Adam (Mid. Tan. Chayyei Sarah, 58b).

*Lustrous hair:* The Talmud (Eiruv. 18a) states that God plaited Eve's hair before bringing her to Adam. This may well be the origin of Rabbinic Judaism's perception of a woman's hair as her 'crowning glory' and therefore to be kept concealed to all but her own husband. A more specific reason – though hardly complimentary to women – is also found in the Midrash (See Ber. Rabb. 17 (13): 'Why do men go with hair uncovered and women with hair covered? It may be compared to one who has committed a crime and is ashamed before people. Therefore women go out with hair covered (as a token of shame for the punishment that Eve brought upon Adam).'

10:1 *You'll love and hold*: Rabbinic tradition has it that Adam and Eve were created as twenty year olds, that is, of marriageable age. Hence, God's first act after Creation was to bring her to Adam (Gen. 2:22), 'like a parent bringing a daughter to the marriage canopy' (Ber. Rab. 8 [15]).

11:2 *When you sow you'll reap:* See Gen. 2:15.

## Garden of Eden

11:3 *Eden:* The name Eden means 'pleasure,' 'luxuriance,' on account of the delectable fruits that it yielded in abundance. This reinforces the greed of Adam and Eve, in finding themselves unable to resist the fruit of that one forbidden tree.
    *Crafted by my hand:* See Gen. 2:8.

*11:4 River Pishon flows with gold:* See Gen. 2:11.
    *Pearls and onyx:* See Gen. 2:12.
    *River Gihon circles Cush:* See Gen. 2:13. Cush is usually identified with Ethiopia.
    *Tigris…Euphrates:* See Gen. 2:14.

12:1 *Have I created for your pleasure:* This and the stanzas that follow, suggesting that man is the centre of the universe and that everything was created with man in mind, were inspired by the following Midrash:

> When God created Adam, he took him on a tour of all the trees of the Garden of Eden, telling him, "See how beautiful and perfect are my creations. I have made them exclusively for you. Pay attention, however, that you do not spoil or destroy my world, for if you do, there will be none other to repair it after you' (Mid. Kohelet. Rab. 9 [4]).

This two thousand year old ecological warning is only now being taken seriously by the developed countries, with rather belated steps to save the planet. Judaism's ancient sages were so ahead of their times on this matter.

12:4 *Yet wishing you could be heaven-bound:* This is intended as an evocation of the later attempt of the generation of the Tower of Babel to build a structure, 'whose top is in the heavens' (Gen. 11:3).

13:1 *A gated Garden:* See Gen. 3:24, where, after Adam's banishment, God stations Cherubim, with fiery swords, at an entrance on the east side of the Garden of Eden.

13:6 *The trees of knowledge and of life:* We have included the tree of (everlasting) life in the initial prohibition, on the basis of Gen. 2:9, which singles out those two trees from all the others that were created, and of Gen. 3:22, which explains the purpose of Adam's banishment as a precaution, 'lest he take also from the tree of life, and eat and live forever.' It remains curious that the latter was not included in the original prohibition.

14:1 *Now you've dominion:* Gen. 1:29-30 clearly express the notion of man's dominion. This was never intended, however, to imply exploitation at the expense of nature, but only enjoyment of renewable resources.

## Lilith and the Serpent

14:3 ff. The legend of Lilith – the primeval temptress – was already referred to by the prophet Isaiah in his enumeration of the spirits and beasts of prey that would lay waste the lands of those who waged war on Israel: 'And the wild cats shall meet with the jackals, and the satyr shall call to his neighbour...and the night monster (*Lilith*) shall repose there' (34:14). There are many references to her in Babylonian demonology, as well as in Talmud, Midrash and Kabbalistic literature.

The Talmud (Eiruvin 18b), for example, commenting on the verse, 'Adam lived one hundred and thirty years, and begat after his own image and likeness,' states that, 'from here we may infer that before he reached that age – and while he was under divine censure – he did not produce offspring who were "after his own image and likeness," but rather, spirits, shades and *Liliths*.'

In another Talmudic passage (Shabb.151b), young men are warned not to sleep in a house alone, lest they be seized and seduced by Lilith. Women in childbirth and newly-born babes were also considered to be in particular danger from her spells, and several medieval works enumerate those dangers and describe measures that might be taken in order to neutralize her violence.

In some medieval Midrashic traditions, Lilith is depicted as having been the consort of Adam after his separation from Eve, following their sin. In other myths, she is actually his first wife – the first Eve – created from the earth at the same time as Adam. We have placed her in the context of the first of these traditions, and chronicled her initial attempt – with the aid of a Serpent that she created by means of her occult arts – to remove Eve from the scene in order to make Adam her own.

The notion of her having created the Serpent was inspired by the widespread belief that Lilith could transform herself or others into any shape or form. Varieties of those Lilith forms are portrayed in primitive art work on Aramaic Incantation Bowls dating back to the 5th cent. BCE. Rashi (on Exod. 4:24) quotes the Mid. Shemot Rab. 5 [8] to the effect that the angel who sought to kill Moses and Zipporah's son, because he was not circumcised, indirectly indicated to Zipporah that particular cause of the divine displeasure by transforming himself into a Serpent. The reptile first wrapped its mouth around the child's head up unto its thigh, and then did the same from the legs up, as far as its genitals, thereby drawing direct attention to the part of the body that required ritual attention.

As myths were handed down orally, it was inevitable that individual elements within the stories would be changed, interchanged or distorted. Hence the Talmud depicts the Serpent as saying, "I shall kill Adam and marry Eve" (Tal. Sota 9b). I have dipped into several of the ingredients of the above Midrashic and legendary sources to create my own version of events, wherein it is Lilith who desires to marry Adam, and who creates the Serpent to aid her efforts.

14:3 *Spirit of the night*: The name Lilith is a variety of the Hebrew word *layla*, meaning 'night'. Spirits were believed to be creatures of the night, performing their demonic arts and striking their foes in the darkness, the element wherein they thrived. It should not be forgotten that already in the Bible, Esau's shadowy adversary – according to tradition, his counterpart in the world of the spirits (*Saro shel Esav*) – begged Jacob to let him return to his place, 'since day had already dawned' (Gen. 32:27). See our note on 115:1, below).

15:1 The notion of Eve's extended wandering around the Garden was inspired by Mid. Ber. Rab. 19 [3], which states that God took Adam on a sight-seeing trip throughout the world and through time, showing him the fertile and arid regions, and countries of dense and sparse habitation. It was while Adam was away on that fact-finding mission that, according to the Midrash, the Serpent carried out his mission to entice Eve to eat of the forbidden fruits.

I have slightly inverted this tradition, sending Eve away on such a mission, to enable Lilith to entice Adam.

15:3 *And with him to cleave*: Ancient rabbinic tradition has it that the Serpent's purpose in enticing Eve was to claim her for itself, and as part of that plan he sought to kill Adam (See Tal. Sota 9b). We have adapted that idea, making the Serpent a mere instrument of Lilith's desire.

## Eating of the Forbidden Fruit

17:4 *Without so much as the slightest touch*: God's original command to Adam was exclusively that he desist from eating the fruit of the forbidden tree, with no hint of any prohibition against touching it (See Gen. 2:17). According to Midrashic tradition, Eve, by extending the prohibition in this way (See Gen.3:3), enabled the Serpent to prove to her that just as she was in error on that score, so was she in error regarding any divine punishment for eating of it.

18:2 *So if, in touching, all was well*: See previous note.

18:3 *That was really nice*: See Gen. 3:6.

*And, beholding his sheer bliss*: It is curious that Adam puts up no resistance to Eve's request that he eat of the forbidden fruit. Our reading of Gen. 3:6 brings out the force of the word *immah*, 'together with her,' in the phrase 'She gave also to her husband [who was] together with her (*immah*), that he ate.' We regard that word as connoting an act of intimacy which rendered Adam insensitive to the full implication of his act.

18:5 *Whose shame for them had not been known*: See Gen. 2: 25.

18:7 See Gen. 3:11.

19:1 *She desired the pleasures fleeting*: See Gen. 3:12.

19:3 *A victim of the serpent's ruse*: See Gen. 3:13.

19:5 *I've brought you fig leaves*: See Gen. 3:21.

19:7 *What have you done now?*: See Gen. 3:14.

*To live in peace with the man I'd made*: The implication of the biblical text is that, before this 'enmity' (See Gen. 3:15) was imposed, man and serpent lived in a state of peaceful co-existence.

20:1 *Now, through you, Eve has sinned*: A curious Talmudic tradition has it that the serpent raped Eve and 'injected into her a (moral) poison' whose effect, as far as Israel was concerned, was only neutralised through the divine revelation at Sinai (See Tal. Av. Zar. 22b).

20:5 *In clearing, weeding, pruning – and pain*: See Gen. 3:17.
*As thorns and thistles tear at his skin*: See Gen. 3:18.
　　*Those he will name Seth, Cain and Abel*: See Gen. 4:1,2,25.

20:6 *Your pain will be great when you give birth*: See Gen. 3:16.
　　*He'll be the one to give the commands*: Ibid.

20:7 *He'll strike your head; you'll bite his toe*: See Gen. 3:15. The Midrash (See Yalkut Shim'oni 3 (29) ) states that God's original purpose was to make the serpent king of all the animals, to have it walk erect and enable it to enjoy human food. His rebellion against God, however, was punished measure for measure: He was hitherto to become 'the most accursed of all beasts' (Gen. 3:14); he was to walk on his belly and eat dust throughout his life (ibid.).

21:2 *Wielding a sword constantly turning*: See Gen. 3:24.

21:3 *And have to provide for his own needs*: See Gen. 3:19.

## Cain and Abel

22:2 *Twin sisters were born with Abel and Cain*: The Midrash, perhaps attempting to explain how Adam and Eve's sons managed to procreate, asserts that twin sisters were born together with them, and that, in an age before incest was prohibited, they were designated to be their respective wives. But that tradition gets even more exotic when it adds that an extra twin sister was born with Abel. That sister became the subject of a furious dispute between the brothers, with Cain asserting his right to her as the firstborn son, and consequently entitled to a double portion of any family inheritance (See Deut. 21:17). Abel argued that the fact that she was born together with him proves that she was his intended (This wife/sister tradition actually has its roots in ancient Babylonian family law, and is employed to add a measure of moral justification to Abraham's having passed off his wife, Sarah, to both the Egyptians (See Gen. 12:13) and to the Philistine king, Avimelech (See Gen. 20:2), as his sister. In ancient Near Eastern mythology, the goddess Anath was both the sister and wife of Baal.).

22:3 *The fattest lambs…devotedly procured*. See Gen. 4:4.

23:1 *From now you are exiled!*: See Gen. 4:12.

23:4 *The sister whom he chose*: The Bible refers to Adam and Eve begetting sons and daughters (See Gen. 5:4). An ancient tradition, preserved in the post-Biblical book of Jubilees, has it that they had a total of nine other children, among whom were two daughters, Awan and Azura, whom Cain and Seth, respectively, married. That source makes no reference to the name of Abel's sister-wife, assuming, perhaps, that he was killed by Cain before he had the opportunity to marry her. Midrashic tradition, on the other hand, credits Abel with having married twin sister-wives. This is based on the duplication of the direct object, *et*, 'together with', in the phrase *et achiv et Havel* ('[And she went on to give birth to (a child) **together with** his brother, (and another) **together with** Abel') in Gen. 4:2 (See Ber. Rabb. 22 (3) and Rashi on Gen. 4:2).

Our speculation that Cain's murder of his brother was motivated by his desire for Abel's wife, and that God's selection of Abel's sacrifice and rejection of Cain's was a secondary source of conflict – perhaps 'the last straw that broke the camel's back' – derives directly from that sister-wife conflict situation.

24:3 *And smashed it over Abel's head*: Midrashic tradition has it that the murder weapon was a stone (See Ber. Rabb. 22 (18)).

25:2 *But the ground…will no longer yield its crop*: See Gen. 4:12.

*I've placed a sign between your eyes…Seven-fold shall their punishment be*: See Gen. 4:15.

## Noah and the Ark

26:2 *He even extended…six or seven-fold his lifespan*: Gen. ch. 5 lists the amazing longevity of the antediluvians. Ch. 6:3 describes the reduction of that to a maximum of one hundred and twenty years as a result of human degeneracy.

26:3 *Ten generations on*: Rabbinic tradition states that there were ten generations between Adam and Noah and ten generations between Noah and Abraham (See Ethics of the Fathers 5:2, 3).

27:3-4 *Idols of silver…Men lie with their neighbour's wife*: Such degeneracy is derived in Jewish tradition from the implication of the verse: 'And God saw the earth and behold it was corrupted, for *all flesh* had corrupted its way upon the earth' (Gen. 6:12).

28:4 *The lowest storey is the store*: Of the three storeys referred to in Gen. 6:16, rabbinic tradition had it that the lowest was utilised as a food store, the middle for animal habitation, and the top deck as living quarters for Adam and his family.

28:5 *Will one hundred years suffice?* The extended period that was granted to Noah to make his ark was in order that people might come from far and wide to see it under construction and that they might question Noah as to its purpose, what sin had prompted it and how they might avoid the impending doom (See Rashi on Gen. 6:14). None, however, took Noah's admonition and dire warnings to heart.

The Bible does not tell us how long it took Noah to build his ark. We first encounter him at the age of 500 years (See Gen. 5:32), and it would seem that shortly afterwards he was given his mission, and was 600 years old when he entered the ark. The Midrash assumes that it took 120 years (See Rashi on 6:14), though this might well be merely a rounded number.

31:2 *God sent some lions:* This is a Midrashic tradition (See Ber. Rabb. 32 (14).

## Life in the Ark

31:3 *Had to sacrifice their rest:* The Midrash (See Ber. Rabb. 31; Tanch. Sidra Noach, 15a) asserts that throughout the entire year that Noah and his family spent in the ark, none of them slept, neither by day or night, so busy were they providing food for the animals at the precise hour to which they had been accustomed to eat.

31:4 *The lions called for their food at dawn:* The Midrash (*loc. cit.*) states that, on one occasion, Noah was late in providing the lion with its meal, wheupon it struck out at him and lamed his leg.

32:7 *Six hundred years of age:* See Gen. 8:13.

## 'Testing the Waters'

33:3 *One hundred and fifty days elapsed:* See Gen. 8:3–5.

33:5 *The raven flew back and forth:* See Gen. 8:6–7.

33:6 *Another seven days ensued:* This is not stated in the text, but commentators infer it from 8:10.

*And Noah dispatched a dove:* The Bible does not record what ultimately happened to the raven. The Midrash records that, on one of its sorties on

Noah's behalf, it alighted upon a corpse on the top of a high hill. Instead of returning to the ark to deliver its report, it gorged itself on its prey, prompting Noah to replace it with a dove which kept faithfully to its mission (See Mid. Yalkut Shimoni ch.8).

34:2 *To the family's great relief*: See 8:11.

34:5 *Will multiply like fish*: See Gen. 8:17; 9:7.

34:6 *To the foot of Mount Ararat*: See Gen.8:4.

35:1 *And recognise his worth*: See Gen.9: 11-17.

## Noah's Last Days

35:2 *Noah lived the good life*: See Gen. 9:1.
   *Planting many vine*: See Gen. 9:20.
   *And downing his fine wine*: See Gen. 9:21.

35:3 *His grandson, Canaan, peeped in*: Following the view of the Midrash and some modern commentators, we have made Canaan, Noah's grandson, the initial 'peeping Tom', rather than his father Ham. Only in this way can we explain why, when Noah awakens, sobers up and discovers what indignity he was subjected to, he directs the full force of his condemnation toward Canaan (See Gen. 9:25-26), rather than Ham. To maintain the biblical account, those sources assume that, having stared at his grandfather, Canaan calls his father, Ham, who also made no effort to cover up his father's nakedness, but merely reported the situation to his brothers.

It is significant that the text states that 'Noah realised what his youngest son *had done to him* (Gen.9:24). This suggests an act perpetrated on Noah and related to his nakedness. Taken together with the fact that in Biblical language 'to see, or uncover, the nakedness' of a person connotes a sexual act (See Lev. 20:11, 17-21), and we have a strong indication that it was an act of homosexual rape that had occurred. This is in line with a Midrashic tradition (Ber. Rabb. 36 (7) that Ham castrated his father.

## Tower of Babel

36:5 *Living in one place*: The biblical story of the Tower of Babel is a highly condensed version, contained within a mere nine verses (Gen. 11:1-9), and omitting the names of any leaders of the revolt against heaven. It depicts the entire human race, offspring of Noah, as living in one area after the flood. Their nomadic existence eventually leads them to 'the Land of Shinar where they settled down (v.2)'. Shinar is identified with Babylonia, which embraced the lands of Akkad and Sumer (See Gen.10:10–11), the north and south of the country, respectively.

37:1 *It was a sacred tongue*: Jewish tradition takes it for granted that the original language spoken by Adam, and with which he communicated with God, was Hebrew. 'Our biblical story views the disruption of communication between human beings as the consequence of man's placing himself in disharmony with God' (Nahum. M. Sarna, *The JPS Torah Commentary, Genesis* (JPS., N.Y., 1989), p.81.)

*To teach right from wrong*: The reference here is to the language of the Torah, given centuries later at Sinai.

37:2 *Shinar*: Hebraised form of Babylonian Sumer. It occurs again later, in the episode of the battle of the four kings against the five in which Abraham became embroiled (See Gen. 14:1). The leader of the former confederacy was Amraphel, king of Shinar.

37:3 *The heavens come close to touching earth*: The Midrash (Ber. Rabb. 38 (2) states that some of the Sodomites believed that once every 1,656 years the firmament disintegrated. They therefore suggested that it be supported with pillars at the north, south and west, and with their own structure, the tower, to the east. The origin of this curious tradition is obscure, as is the precise objective of that structural activity. We may conjecture that, according to the Midrash, the shallow, disintegrating firmament could more easily be penetrated to the east by the tower.

37:7 *Exactly as told*: See Gen. 11:3.

38:4 *He was handed a scraper or a yard stick*: This is based on Midrashic tradition (Ber. Rabb. 38 (15).

38:6 *God scattered the rebels all over the globe*: See Gen. 11:8.

## Abram discovers God

39:2 *Born to Terach in the city of Ur*: Ur is referred to in the book of Genesis as *Ur Kasdim*, Ur of the Chaldees. The Chaldeans settled in that area around 900 BC. They were great builders and created the great ziggurat, still standing, of Nanna, a man-made structure with a temple at its summit. Ur was the hub of the Sumerian civilisation. The meaning of his name is *Av* ('father') *ram* ('exalted'), a reference to his role as 'exalted father' of the Israelite nation. His more universal concerns, to wean all men to monotheism, prompted God to change his name later to Avraham, which the Bible itself explains to mean 'father of the multitude' (see Gen. 17:4-5). He is believed to have lived between 2166 and 1990 BCE.

39:3 *Nimrod, king of Chaldea*: See previous note. The 1st century historian, Josephus, as well as Talmud and Midrash, regarded Nimrod as the monarch who designed and oversaw the building of the Tower of Babel. He is also identified with Amraphel king of Shinar who was one of the confederacy against which Abram waged war (See Gen. 14:1 and our note on p.50:6 below), as well as with Hammurabi. Their mutual hostility, according to those Jewish sources, would clearly have dated back, therefore, to Abram's childhood when he denounced the idolatry of the country and influenced people toward monotheism.

40:2–43:5 This tradition, of Abram smashing his father's idols to make him realise the folly of his belief in their divinity, is found in the Midrash (See Ber. Rabb. 38 (13)), and is one of the first stories taught to young Jewish schoolchildren when they commence their religious education.

43:4 *After four hundred years of exile*: See Gen. 15:13.
   *Crowning kings by River Gihon*: King Solomon was crowned on the banks of the Gihon river (See I Kings 1:33, 38, 45). Rivers were considered happy auguries of a perennial and tranquil reign; although Gihon, having been one of the four original rivers that issued forth from the Garden of Eden (See Gen.2:13), presumably conveyed the symbolic vindication of the monarch's right to rule in accordance with divine purpose from the very beginning of time.

## Abram and the Promised Land

44:2 *He seeks your life for impugning his faith*: The Midrash (See Ber. Rabb. 38 (13)) describes how Nimrod arrested Abram and presented him with the choice of either worshipping the natural elements, whose divinity Abram had already tested and found wanting, or be thrown into a fiery furnace:

   'Worship the Fire!' commanded Nimrod. 'Why should I not rather worship the water which extinguishes the fire?' replied Abram. 'Then worship the water!' said Nimrod. 'Why should I not rather worship the cloud which carries the water?' 'Then worship the cloud!' retorted Nimrod. 'Would it not be better to worship the powerful wind which scatters the clouds?' 'So worship the wind!' said Nimrod. 'But what about the human beings who have the power to insulate themselves against the wind?' said Abram.

Exasperated, Nimrod said, 'I bow to none but the fire. I shall now cast you into it, and we'll see if the God whom you worship has the power to save you from it!' They cast Abraham into the furnace, but he survived.

45:1 *But in Canaan, there you'll grow*: The sentiment expressed in this and the previous stanza is inspired by Gen. 12: 1-2, 'Go for yourself,' and the comment of Rashi (*ad loc*): 'For your own benefit and that of your posterity'.

45:3 *Abram called on the men of the town*: The abstruse phrase, '[Abram took with him] the souls *he had made* in Haran' (Gen. 12:5) is explained by the Midrash (Ber. Rab. Ch 39; See also Rashi on 12:5) as follows: 'The reference here is to those whom he had brought under the divine wing; for Abram converted the men while Sarah converted the women. Hence Scripture regards it as if they had actually "made" – that is, given birth to – those people.'

45:5 *Inviting everyone in to feast*: Abra(ha)m is the symbol of hospitality in Jewish tradition, as exemplified by the episode of the three wayfarers he invited into his home, and the great effort he and Sarah went to in order to provide them with the choicest fare (See Gen. chap.18). This is thrown into even greater relief by Talmudic tradition (See Tal. B.M. 86a) which states that this particular act of hospitality took place on the third day after his circumcision, when his pain was at its most acute.

## Sarai in Peril

46:3 *So Abram and Sarai left for Egypt*: See Gen. 12:10.

46:6 *Say you are my sister*: See notes 22:2 and 23:4.

47:6 *A fearful pain gripped him*: See Gen.12:17.

47:7 *Stricken in their phallus*: Verse 17 includes 'his household' in those 'severely smitten' together with Pharaoh. The Midrash (Ber. Rabb. 42 (2) infers from that that they were smitten with the identical pox, which it identifies with *ra'atan,* a debilitating skin disease which makes intercourse excruciatingly painful.

48:4 *That she wasn't quite so smart:* Suffice to say that there is no biblical warrant for our assertion that they were sent away with gifts, though v.16 implies that Pharaoh had lavished gifts of livestock on Abram at the time he seized Sarai. That Hagar was of Egyptian nationality is attested to in Gen. 16:1, though the notion that she was planted 'as a snare' is, of course, pure speculation!

## Abraham and Lot

48:5 *Now the flocks...increased each passing week:* See Gen. 13:5

49:2 *Trampling...and devouring their yields:* The Midrash (Ber. Rabb. 41(6)) states that Abram's animals were all muzzled to avoid their wandering off and grazing in other people's fields, whereas Lot's were deliberately led onto private property. When Abram's shepherds chided Lot's for perpetrating theft, the latter answered, 'Did not God tell our master's uncle, Abram, "To your seed shall I give this whole land"? Since he has no offspring, when he dies our master, Lot, will assuredly inherit this entire land, so we are within our rights to allow our flocks to graze wherever they wish!'

50:3 *A book and a sword:* This phrase is based on the Midrashic statement (See Sifri on Parashat Eikev) that, 'At the Sinaitic revelation, the Book (of the Torah) and a sword descended bound together from heaven.' The message was that neglect of Torah's moral and ethical values will bring with it national self-destruction.

## Wars of the Kings

50:5 *To recruit three hundred men:* The precise number of fighting men recruited and trained by Abram is given as 318 (See Gen. 14:14), all 'born of his household,' that is offspring of his slaves. They were considered more loyal and trustworthy than those recruited from outside as mercenaries.

50:6 *Under Amraphel, the Babylonian king:* Amraphel was traditionally identified with the famous law-maker, Hammurabi, though this is widely discounted by modern scholars (See our note on 39:3).

*And the four chieftains under his wing:* This episode is popularly referred to as 'the battle of the four kings'. It highlights the courage, wealth and influence of Abram that he could defeat a formidable confederacy that had just won such a decisive battle. It also underscores Abram's noble character in that, notwithstanding his nephew's waywardness and estrangement from him, Abram did not hesitate for a moment after being told that his nephew had been captured, but immediately raised an army to rescue him. In later Judaism, the act of *pidyon shivuyyim*, rescuing kidnapped coreligionists, is a cardinal duty, to raise funds for which one may even sell a scroll of the sacred Torah.

51:4 *Though the king appeared displeased*: See vv. 22–24. In ancient and modern Middle Eastern society, it is regarded as the greatest insult, tantamount to a rebuff and rejection of friendship, to refuse gifts that are proffered.

## Sarai and Hagar

52:2 *By God's good grace:* See Gen. 16: 1-2.

52:4 *I was blessed by God to procreate:* This proud boast is found in the Midrash (Ber. Rabb. 45 (4).

54:5 *Which the other, by force, shall deny:* That Israel's future suffering at the hands of Ishmael would be a measure of retribution for Sarai's treatment of Hagar is suggested by the classical commentator, Moses ben Nachman (*Nachmanides*) in his commentary to Gen. 16:6. When that 13th century authority spoke of Ishmael, he was referring to the militant Islam of his day. His prognostication regarding Israel's future oppression at Islamic hands is nothing short of prophetic.

## Visit of the three Angels

57:1 *Which Abraham thought quite odd*: Abraham would have been disconcerted by this lapse of moral convention by a strange male visitor to the home asking about the whereabouts of its mistress. A married woman would not normally fraternise with other men, but remain in the inner recesses of her tent. Hence Abraham's pointed reply, 'Behold, she is in her tent!' (v.9.).

57:6 *The second angel had a task:* The Talmud (B.M. 86b) asserts that these three angels, Michael, Raphael and Gabriel, each had a specific task to perform, since God only entrusts one task at a time to his angels. Michael was to deliver the news of Sarah's pregnancy; Raphael was to heal Abraham following his circumcision and Gabriel was charged with overseeing the destruction of Sodom and Gomorrah.

## Sodom and Gomorrah

58:1 *To total lawlessness*: Talmudic sources provide many examples of the wickedness of the inhabitants of Sodom and Gomorrah and their total insensitivity to, and rejection of, basic moral norms. They credit the Sodomites with having issued a ban on extending hospitality to any visitor on pain of death. But they went further and enforced this by terrorising any such visitor. They strapped him to a bed. If he was too short for it, they would stretch him until he fitted; if he was too long for it , they would sever his feet accordingly.

Another tradition had it that acts of charity were punishable by death. Thus, if a poor man came to town, and begged alms, they would readily give him a dinar note on which they wrote their names, but they would not give him even a morsel of bread or a drop of water. After he had collapsed and died, they would retrieve their dinar notes from his pocket. Once, they heard that a young girl had fed bread to a wayfarer, so they smothered her body with honey and tied her down to the roof of a building where the bees stung her to death (Bem. Rabb. 9 (24); Tal. San. 108b–109a).

One may conjecture that all those 'traditions' were inspired by the daily acts of horrific cruelty inflicted on the Jews of ancient Judaea by the Roman occupiers. Public crucifixion, burning at the stake and flogging were daily occurrences. The term 'Sodomite' became applied by the Jews to any cruel and wicked person (See Mid. Ber. Rabb. 41 (10)).

58:4 *Morality was excised:* This might explain why Lot instinctively offers his own two daughters to the mob in exchange for the lives of his guests (See Gen. 19: 7-8).

59:1 *With the wicked pass away?:* See Gen. 18:22-23.

60:3 *From my own cherished friend:* Abraham is indeed referred to by God as 'my friend' (See Is. 41:8).

60:5 *Go home, they're all unsaved:* Abraham's expostulation with God throws up a number of philosophical problems, and, at one level, exposes the immaturity of his perception of God's justice. For, had Abraham possessed implicit faith in that justice, he could never have chided 'the judge of the entire earth' with 'judging unjustly' (Gen. 18:25). Was it not also an act of conceit on Abraham's part to imagine that his own moral conscience was more sensitive than God's?

Nahum Sarna raises some further issues:

'More complicated is his second request that the entire city be spared for the sake of an innocent minority...Indirectly it asserts that there is a greater infraction of justice in the death of an innocent few than in allowing a guilty majority to escape retribution; it assumes that the merit of a minority is powerful enough to overcome the wickedness of the majority. These are major themes in later biblical literature because divine mercy can also be divine toleration of evil. A problem of serious dimensions to prophet and sage alike. (N.Sarna, *op.cit.*, p.133).

Germane to this issue is the bestowal on Abraham's offspring of the blessing of land, numerous progeny and prosperity as a reward for 'his having listened to My voice and kept My charge: My commandments, My laws and My teachings' (Gen. 26:5). This assumes that, notwithstanding the merit or otherwise of his descendants, one man's righteousness may 'cover up all transgressions!' To both complicate and resolve this particular dilemma, it has to be said that, later in the Pentateuch, Israel's prosperity and occupation of the Promised Land is made conditional upon its observance of divine law (See Lev. 26:3-41; Deut. 4:25ff; 6:12-17, 11;13-17, *et al.*).

## Lot and the Destruction of the Cities

61:1 *Invited them to his home*: On Sodom's attitude to hospitality, see our comment to p. 58:1. Against that background it is difficult to explain why Lot was prepared to endanger his own life by welcoming the two angels into his home. We may conjecture that due to his upbringing in the home of Abraham, which witnessed a steady in-flow of visitors, hospitality remained instinctive in his character. Perhaps it was that single merit which secured his and his family's deliverance, in that Judaism believes that one cannot measure the relative value of individual good deeds. This is enunciated in one of its most popular ethical texts, *Pirkei Avot* ('Ethics of the Fathers'): 'Be as meticulous in the observance of a minor precept as a major one, for you do not know the reward for each precept' (2:1). As regards the specific precept of extending hospitality, Judaism regards it as greater than going to receive the divine Presence. This is inferred from the fact that Abraham broke off in the middle of a divine visitation in order to run and invite the three wayfarers to his home (See Gen.18:1).

63:1 *And Gomorrah brimstone and fire*: This devastation is referred to once again, in Deut. 29:22, as the punishment that will be meted out for the sin of idolatry.

63:3 *And she was preserved...as a pillar:* The 1st century historian, Josephus, claims to have actually seen that pillar of salt (See *Antiquities* 1 (203). Current claims for its identification are mere conjecture.

## Lot and his daughters

64:2 *And let him be seduced:* The daughters knew that their father, when sober, would never willingly have agreed to such an act of incest.

64:4 *Moab...Ben-Ami*: Ben-Ami is stated to have been the progenitor of Ammon. (See Gen. 19:38). Both Moab and Ammon, descendants of Lot and his daughters, inhabited adjoining territory on Israel's eastern border. Throughout the Biblical period, a constant state of war existed between them both and Israel.

## Isaac and Ishmael

65:1 *Believing in God and in his own mission:* That Isaac was the spiritual heir of Abraham is inferred by the Talmud (B.M. 87a) from the verse, 'These are the generations of Isaac, son of Abraham; Abraham begat Isaac' (Gen. 25:19). The unnecessary repetition of the statement is understood to teach that Isaac was both his biological and spiritual son.

65:2 *But Ishmael, his big brother:* The birth of Ishmael had taken place some thirteen years earlier (See Gen.16:15-16) when Abraham was 86 years old.

65:3 *'You worship a God,' mocked Ishmael:* The Midrash (Ber. Rabb. Ch.53) credits Ishmael not merely with a lack of faith, but with an immersion in idolatry, for which reason Sarah was determined to banish him from her home.

The precise danger that Ishmael posed to Isaac is, however, difficult to determine given that it hinges on the vague word, *metzachek*, in the verse, 'Sarah saw the son whom Hagar had borne to Abraham *metzachek* with Isaac, so she said to Abraham, 'Cast out that slave-woman and her son...'(Gen.21: 8–9). The Midrash points to the occurrence of that identical word variously, in the sense of idolatry (See Exod. 32:6), murder (See II Sam. 2:14) and immorality (See Gen. 39:17). They consequently attribute any or all of those acts to Ishmael as the cause of his banishment. In our version we have generally alluded to his degenerate life.

## Binding of Isaac

67:5 *Mankind was entitled to observe his resolve*: This rationale of the test of Abraham is provided by the medieval commentator Moses b.Nachman (*Nachmanides*). He states that one cannot compare potential righteousness — with which Abraham was undoubtedly invested — with actual righteousness, that is one that has actually been put to the test, and which has been publicly acclaimed. Hence, reluctantly, God had to impose the *Akedah* (binding) test upon him, justifying thereby all the reward he had already showered upon him and which he had promised to bestow on his offspring (See *Commentary of RMBN* to Gen. 22:1).

68:2 *The one that you both love more*: The designation of Isaac as 'the son that you both love more' occurs in Gen. 22:2, where God summons Abraham to 'take your son, your only one, the one you love, Isaac.' the Midrash (Ber. Rabb. 55 (7) views this unnecessarily expansive designation of Isaac as representing the key words of an exchange between God and Abraham:

> God originally said to Abraham: 'Take you son.' Abraham replied, 'I have two sons'. God replied, 'your only one,' to which Abraham responded, 'one of them (Isaac) is the "the only one" of his mother (Sarah) and the other (Ishmael) is also "the only one" of his mother (Hagar).' God therefore clarified it even further: "the one you love," to which Abraham retorted, 'but I love them both.' Finally, God had to spell it out unequivocally: "Isaac".

As to why God did not state at the outset, 'Take Isaac,' The Midrash (Ber. Rabb. 55 (7)) suggests that it was in order not to shock Abraham, but to break the news to him gradually and gently (see next note), or it was to make the divine instruction precious in his eyes, and to grant him extra reward for every word exchanged.

68:3 *Insisting it must be Satan's work*: This allusion to 'Satan's work' was inspired by the Midrashic references to his part in the unfolding of the events of the *Akedah*. One such reference has it that Satan did his utmost to frustrate Abraham's mission and cause him to lose divine grace. Thus, he is said to have blocked Abraham's progress to the *Akedah* by transforming himself into a river. Abraham walked forward into it until the water reached his nose, at which point God intervened and removed the obstacle. The death of Sarah, referred to immediately after Abraham returned from the *Akedah* (Ge.23:1), is also attributed to Satan who abruptly revealed to her that her husband had taken their son and killed him (Mid. Tanch, chap. 22).

68:6 *The lamb God always provides*: See Gen. 22:8.

72:2 *'The princess'*: A reference to the literal meaning of the name Sarah.

*Israel's foremost matriarch*: The other three traditional matriarchs of Israel are Rebeccah, Rachel and Leah.

## Purchase of the cave of Machpelah

72:4 *Refused to deal with strangers*: This is our rationale for the fact that Abraham, instead of appealing directly to Ephron, felt constrained to ask some influential Hittite men to intercede on his behalf with their chief.

73:3 *The two-layered cave*: The Hebrew name of the cave, *Machpelah* (Gen. 23:9), is derived from the word *kefel*, meaning 'double'. The Talmud (Eiruv. 53a) explains the origin of the name as derived from the 'pairs', or couples buried there, namely Adam and Eve, Abraham and Sarah, Isaac and Rebeccah, and Jacob and Leah.

*I've silver coins of perfect mint*: This is based upon Abraham's assurance to the Hittite intercessors that he will pay to Ephron 'silver coins of the highest value' (Gen. 23:9). This is reinforced at the end of the transaction: 'And Abraham paid Ephron…coins acceptable to any merchant' (Gen. 23:16, and our penultimate stanza).

73:4 *His parlous financial state*: This has no basis in the text; yet we offer it as an attempt to explain Ephron's unexpected readiness to part with tribal land.

73:6 *Take it as a gift*: It was probably a convention among those desert tribes – as it was in later Arab communities – that any request made by a guest in one's home or community had to be readily fulfilled. In practice, this did not prevent the host from exacting compensation, and more, at a later date!

## A Wife for Isaac

75:1 *Eliezer of Damascus*: Nowhere, throughout this lengthy episode, is the name of 'the servant' (the designation used throughout) disclosed. Rabbinic tradition identifies it, however, with 'Eliezer, the steward of his house,' referred to in Gen. 15:2. He is described there as *damesek Eliezer*, Eliezer from Damascus.

75:3 *With finding for him a wife*: The episode is introduced by the statement that 'Abraham was by now well-advanced in years' (Gen. 24:1). This explains why he sent a trusted servant on this most important mission, rather than undertake the journey himself. The solemn oath he imposed on Eliezer, adjuring him 'by the Lord, God of heaven and God of earth, not to take a wife from among the Canaanites…' (v.3) is indicative of his attitude toward the moral degeneracy of the Canaanites. Such an antipathy toward them may well have been compacted by the family stories (oral traditions) regarding the original Canaan's indecency, and the curse imposed on him for that by God (See Gen. 9:21ff and our note to p.35:3).

76:1 *So lay your hand upon my knee*: See Gen. 24:2. The Hebrew text actually required the servant to place his hand 'beneath the thigh' of Abraham. 'Thigh seems to be a euphemism for the male organ (cf. Gen. 46:26; Ex. 1:5). Perhaps by touching it, the person swearing the oath calls sterility or loss of children upon himself, should he violate it' (*The Jewish Study Bible*, eds. Adele Berlin and Marc Zvi Brettler, Jewish Publication Society, Oxford University Press, 2003, p. 48 n.2). The symbolism may also have been that the person swearing the oath indicates thereby that his commitment is to fulfil the mission to the letter, as if he himself were the very offspring of Abraham's loins, seeking out the fulfilment of his own destiny.

76:2 *With ten camels and countless gifts*: The verse, 'And God blessed Abraham with all things' (Gen. 24:1) indicates the vast wealth he had accumulated by the end of his life. Aware that Eliezer might encounter difficulty in persuading the girl's family to leave her home and land and journey into the unknown, he felt obliged to send a ten camel cavalcade in order to establish his social and financial standing. That this show of wealth had the desired effect is clear from the fact that Rebekah's brother, Laban, 'ran' to meet Eliezer (See Rashi on Gen. 24:29).

76:4 *The Most High*: N. Sarna (op cit), points out that Eliezer is 'the first person whom Scripture records as praying for personal guidance at a critical moment.'

76:5 *Filling him with ecstasy*: In the biblical account (See v. 27), Eliezer offers up a thanksgiving to God for having answered his plea. The format of his thanks – *Baruch …Adonai Elohai…Avraham asher* ('Blessed be the Lord, God of my master, Abraham, who…') – provided the core formula for the opening blessing of the *Amidah*, the central prayer of Jewish liturgy, and, indeed, of all Hebrew blessings.

77:5 *A crafty, scheming man*: Although in this opening episode Laban's true character is not yet revealed, yet his haste to entertain the wealthy visitor, his attempt to stall Eliezer's request (See v.55) and his later treatment of Jacob, all confirm the traditional image of Laban's character.

78:4 *She'll comfort him for the loss of his mum*: See v. 67.

78:5 *Brother Laban and her mum and dad*: Whereas in v.50 we find Laban and the father, Betuel, acceding to Eliezer's request, yet, but three verses later, Betuel vanishes from the narrative and the gifts are given to Rebekah's 'brother and mother' (v. 53) alone. It is they who also attempt to delay Rebekah's departure 'for up to ten months or a year' (v. 55). Rabbinic tradition, noting Eliezer's reticence to eat the food put before him (See v. 33), suggests that Betuel put poison in Eliezer's food in order to frustrate his plan to take his daughter away, but that an angel switched the plates, resulting in Betuel's sudden demise.

79:3 *Be the matriarch of countless tribes...they shall rout*: See v. 60. This blessing is conferred upon brides at the *bedekken* (veiling) prior to the marriage ceremony.

79:4 *He was praying in a nearby field*: The text states that 'Isaac went to meditate (*lasu'ach*) in the field toward evening' (Gen. 24:63). Rabbinic tradition interprets this, however, as 'sacred meditation' or prayer. While Abraham is credited with having introduced a morning prayer (*Shachrit*), Isaac – whose 'meditations' took place 'toward evening' – is considered the initiator of the regular afternoon prayer (*Minchah*). The third patriarch, Jacob, who 'entreated his God...at night time,' prior to lying down and having his fateful dream of the angels (Gen. 28:11) is the putative originator of the regular night-time service (*Ma'ariv*).

79:5 *She covered her face with a veil*: See v. 65. Covering her face with a veil was both a mark of modesty and an indication of her willingness to become his wife, since married women traditionally donned a veil.

80:2 *No faith in God professed*: Midrashic tradition (Ber. Rabb. 59 (10) has it that Ishmael actually repented his ways toward the end of his life. This is derived from the statement that Abraham completed his life 'old and content' (Gen. 25:8). 'Such a summation of a life is found with no other personality in biblical literature. The phrase describes not his longevity, which is otherwise mentioned, but the quality of his earthly existence' (N Sarna, *op. cit.*, p. 174).

Had the cloud of Ishmael still enveloped him, such a summation would hardly have been appropriate.

## Jacob and Esau

**81:1** *But the years passed with no bundle of joy*: The fact that three out of the four matriarchs had difficulty conceiving – Leah being the exception – is explained by the sages on the grounds that 'the Almighty desires the supplications of the righteous.' From a philosophical standpoint, this 'explanation' provides as many problems as it solves!

**81:3** *That one inside was pursuing the other.* This is based on the phrase, 'And the children struggled within her' (Gen. 25:22).

**81:4** *She went to discern of the Lord, her God*: Rabbinic tradition has it that the founders of the Semitic peoples, Shem and Eber (See Gen. 10:21), were paragons of piety who spent their lives in religious meditation inside an academy of learning (yeshivah), while freely offering help and guidance to people with their personal, spiritual and family problems. Thus, the Midrash explains that Rebekah's journey 'to enquire of the Lord' (Gen. 25:22) was, in fact, to their academy, in order to seek out the help of God through the mediation of those two spiritual giants.

**82:1** Esau...'fully formed': The etymology of the name *Eisav* (Esau) is uncertain. The verb *a-sa-h*, from which it derives, may mean 'to make,' 'to form.' Hence our explanation, 'fully formed,' with an abundance of hair. It may, however, derive from its other meaning of 'to squeeze,' 'compress,' – a reference to the pressure on Rebekah's womb occasioned by his struggle to emerge first.

**82:2** *Jacob – One who pursues with zeal*: The name 'Jacob' (Hebrew, *Ya'akov*) means, literally, 'one who grasps the heel' (of his brother).

**82:3** *Esau hunted...the Jordan and the Sea*: Esau is described as 'a skilful hunter, a man of the outdoors' (Gen. 25:27). The sea referred to here is the Mediterranean.

**82:5** *And studied a large tome:* The existence of such a tome is, of course, entirely in the writer's imagination.

**82:6** *Of prayers...Isaac adored:* This is rooted in the phrase 'Isaac loved Esau (*ki tzayid befiv) because* he hunted (for food) for his (Isaac's) mouth' (Gen. 25:28).

The Midrash, on the other hand, renders the phrase to convey the very opposite sense: 'Isaac loved Esau *although* he hunted (i.e. misled) him with his mouth', namely through utterances that exhibited a false piety. Hence our description of Esau as exaggeratedly reciting prayers to God whenever Isaac was around (See Rashi on v. 28).

## Purchase of the Birthright

83:2 *My life-style…has taken its toll*: Esau was terribly depressed (See Gen. 25:29, 30) and believed he was about to die (see Gen. 25:32). There was clearly a compelling reason for this, as it would hardly have been the natural state of mind of the hunter who flirted with death each day. Our suggestion, that he had been badly wounded by a wild beast, would explain his readiness to part with his birthright, and the financial reward of a double portion of the estate that came with that inheritance, for a mere mess of pottage. At that moment his chief concern would have been for food to replenish his spent energy.

83:4 *With garlic and sausage*: I have adopted poetic licence in this reference to sausage which is certainly anachronistic. The earliest reference to such a casing of meat or blood comes from China around 590 BCE. It is also mentioned by Homer, and seems to have been popular in Greek and Roman society. We have no evidence, however, that it was known in the biblical period.

84:2 *To don priestly robes, with hair unshorn?*: This exchange between the brothers, on the issue of the awesome religious responsibilities imposed on the firstborn, is contained in Rashi's comment on Esau's statement, 'Behold I am going to die' (v. 32). Rashi interprets this as a direct reaction to Jacob's enumeration of all the religious duties incumbent upon the firstborn, for infringement of which the penalty is death.

## Isaac in Adversity and Prosperity

85:1 *Famine-prone Canaan…drove Isaac to seek refuge*: See Gen. 26:1

85:2 *My sister!* See v.7. His father, Abraham, also sought to evade danger by asking Sarah to describe herself as his sister (see Gen. 12:13). The saving of life takes precedence even over the pursuit of truth. In the Song of Songs, the term 'sister' is used to denote one's beloved. On the assumption that this term was applied as early as the patriarchal period, Abraham and Isaac's request may not appear such a blatant falsehood! (See, however, on 46:6, above.)

## Jacob, Esau and the Birthright

88:1 *Isaac was now advanced in years*: Rashi calculates Isaac's age at this time as one hundred and twenty-three (See Rashi on Gen. 27:2).

88:2 *The soul divine returns to its source*: Genesis 27:2 indicates that Isaac was indeed anticipating the approach of death.

88:5 *And my spirits will then soar.* A dispenser of blessing had to be in a happy and benevolent frame of mind. For that reason, later Judaism declared a mourner unable to recite the priestly blessing of the congregation, a highlight of the daily Temple, and subsequent synagogue's, morning service.

89:3 *And dispatch me two young goats*: Rashi suggests that the flavour of a young goat is very similar to that of venison. It is difficult to imagine, however, that Isaac, well accustomed to Esau's regular offering of venison dishes, could possibly have been duped by the substitution of goat's meat. Hence my suggestion that Rebekah camouflaged the goat's meat with a venison sauce.

91:2 *Strange that Esau should invoke God*: We are indebted to Rashi for this slant on Isaac's confusion.

    *That he inwardly reviled*: See our comment above, on 82:6.

91:7 *By erasing the intention of Isaac's mind*: To clarify our reconstruction of the situation: Jacob enters, dressed as Esau. Isaac decides to withhold the blessing from this Esau – in reality, Jacob – and to confer it instead upon the other son (whom he assumes will be Jacob, but who is, in fact, Esau). God is constrained, therefore, to impose a degree of amnesia on Isaac, so that he abandons his plan to withhold from the first petitioner (Jacob) the birthright. The result is that Isaac blesses the real Jacob whole-heartedly.

92:5 *Made his way out…made his way in*: See Gen. 27:30.

    *'Up you get, dad, and eat of my stew'*: The terseness of Esau's opening words to his father is well reflected in the text. See Gen. 27:31.

93:5 *I'm horrified…of selling your birthright*: In the biblical account, Isaac does not, in fact, express any disapproval of Esau's having sold his birthright. Perhaps Isaac did not wish to rub salt into his son's wound.

94:3 *And demand…so perverse*: In the biblical source, Esau does not actually ask his father to cancel Jacob's blessing, knowing that such a request would be futile since God had already been invoked to endorse it. He asks, instead, for any residual blessing that his father might feel it appropriate to confer.

95:4 *And the friend let Rebekah know*: V. 42 states, simply, 'It was told to Rebekah'.

96:1 *Our constant aggravation*: See 27:46.

## The dream of the ladder

97:2 *He alighted at an eerie place*: See Gen. 28:11. The Hebrew, *vayyifga bamakom* (literally, 'He alighted on a place'), may also be translated as, 'And he entreated the Omnipresent'. Understanding it in that way, rabbinic tradition ascribed to Jacob the introduction of the recitation of the evening service. See our note on 79:4, above.

97:3 *He prayed to God and prepared for sleep*: See previous note. Later Judaism evolved a prayer (*Keri'at Shema al ha-mittah*), before lying down to sleep each night.

97:4 *He took twelve stones as a support*: We have incorporated a rabbinic tradition, recorded in the name of R. Judah, that he placed twelve stones under his head, corresponding to the twelve tribes of which he was destined to become the primogenitor.

Another view, that of R. Nehemiah, is that he took only three stones, expressive of his wish that, just as God had bestowed His spirit upon his father, Isaac, and grandfather, Abraham, so would he do for him. Yet a further recorded view is that he took just two stones. This is based upon the phrase, 'And he took of *the stones* of the place.' Since we are not told how many stones there were, we are entitled to assume that the minimum plural, namely two, is implied (See Mid. Ber. Rabb. 68 (13). Targum Onkelos, the officially authorised Aramaic translation in Talmudic times, does not provide any number, whereas another well-established Aramaic translation, Targum Jonathan, states that he took four stones. All this adds up to the clear conclusion that we will never know how many stones he actually took!

97:5 *A translucent celestial team*: See Gen. 28:12-15.

97:6 *Who else could it be?*: See v.13.

98:2 *My Temple shall stand as a beacon of light*: See the reference to 'the house of God' and 'the gate of heaven' in v.17.

98:3 *The first…The rest:* Rabbinic tradition explains the mission of the ascending group of angels as that of having protected Jacob from the time he left his father's home until this time when he was about to leave the borders of the Holy Land. That group, thereupon 'ascended' back to heaven on the completion of their mission. The next group, of descending angels, were coming down to fulfil their mission of protecting him for as long as he remained outside the land of Israel.

98:5 *Into one large slab had now been changed:* This is based on the fact that Gen. 28:8 states that, on awakening from his dream, 'he took the *stone* which he had placed under his head.'

## Approaching Laban's Home

99:3 *And we'll take a peep:* The vulnerability of shepherdesses to sexual harassment is well attested, especially in this situation where they were unable to lift the dead-weight stone cover of the well without the help of several male shepherds. The fact that the latter, after feeding their own flocks, replaced that cover, though knowing full-well that Rachel and her fellow-shepherdesses would shortly arrive, explains Jacob's hostility towards them.

99:4 *Their full quota you scoundrels deny:* See Rashi on v.7.

100:2 *At the amazing strength on display:* See v.10. 'This act Jacob performed single-handedly, experiencing a sudden surge of strength at the sight of Rachel and in the knowledge that he was meeting with his own kith and kin at last' (N. Sarna, *op. cit.*, p. 202).

100:4 *He planted a kiss on her cheeks:* While such a gesture might seem a trifle audacious, bearing in mind that he had only just encountered her, yet the Midrash justifies his conduct in the light of the fact they were cousins. The Midrash states, 'All kissing is frivolity except in three situations: A kiss conferred by one initiating another into a position of greatness, a kiss bestowed on one reunited after a lengthy absence, and a kiss bestowed on a relative' (Mid. Ber. Rabb. 70 (11)).

*And wept tears of joy:* While we have interpreted his tears as expressive of joy at his new-found love, the sages prefer to view them otherwise, either as an expression of sadness and embarrassment that, whereas, when Eliezer had visited this family home to secure his mother Rebekah as a wife for Isaac, he had come with ten camels' load of gifts, he was arriving here empty-handed and as a fugitive. A Midrashic exposition has it that his tears were the result of a prophetic revelation that they would not be buried together in the Cave of Machpelah (See Ber. Rabb. 70 (12)).

101:2 *But you with a mere 'hello!'*: Rashi makes this comment (See his commentary to Gen. 29:13), based on the phrase, 'And he (Laban) ran to meet him'. When Eliezer had first arrived, all those years before, Laban had 'ran to meet him' (See Gen. 24:29), in expectation of rich gifts. He ran once again to meet this newcomer from Canaan, but was frustrated that he had clearly come empty-handed.

102:3 *Whom he'd hitherto ignored*: It strikes one as highly implausible that Jacob would not have immediately recognised that the woman in his bed was not his adored Rachel. The rabbis had a tradition that, knowing Laban's cunning, and suspecting his intention to palm off the homely Leah before Rachel, the latter contrived an ingenious and selfless ruse to prevent her sister being humiliated when she entered the bridal bed. Rachel disclosed to Leah, therefore, some secret signs and gestures that she had previously agreed with Jacob so that he would know that it was her, and not another, being escorted to his bed in the dark (See Tal. Meg. 13b).

103:1 *But* in our place *we don't stoop so low*: See Gen. 29:26. The emphasis, 'in our place' is intended to indicate to Jacob that while, *in his place*, it was clearly acceptable to supplant the older brother – as he, Jacob, had done – yet in Laban's place they have a higher ethical conscience, and would never ride rough-shod over the older child by allowing the younger one to marry first.

103:2 *Once this week's celebration's spent*: A Talmudic tradition ascribes the prohibition of 'merging one religious celebration with another' (*me'arbin simchah b'simcha*), to Laban's decision not to allow the wedding of Jacob to Rachel to take place until the seven days of celebration for his nuptials with Leah were completed (See Ber. Rabb. 70 (18).

103:6 *Rachel grew more bitter*: See Gen. 30:1-2.

## Reuben and the Mandrakes

105:5 *'As you will,' replied the man*: This motif, of a passer-by disclosing the aphrodisiacal property of the mandrake to Reuben, is a figment of my imagination, introduced in order to explain how the young Reuben could possibly have known about intimate marital matters, and particularly about the special properties of the mandrake in this area.

*The ardour of his loins*: The Hebrew term for 'mandrake' is *duda'im*, which is a variant of the word *dodim*, meaning '(potion of) lovers'.

106:2 *As arranged*: The Talmud attributes the fact that Rachel was not destined to lie for all eternity next to Jacob in the Cave of Machpelah to her preparedness so readily to surrender up a night with him in return for the mandrakes. She treated her physical and spiritual intimacy with him with scant respect, in bartering it in an unseemly way for the purely sexual gratification offered by the mandrake. (See Tal. Nid. 31b).

## Farewell to Laban's Home

107:4 *I ask you that – and nothing more*: Jacob did, in fact, succeed in seeing his father before the latter's death (See Gen. 35:27). The death of Rebekah, however, goes unrecorded; and we may infer from the reference to Jacob 'coming to his father at Mamre' (*ibid*), that by then Rebekah had already died.

108:2 *With you on the way*: Jacob's legal status was that of a servant who, by his work, had paid off in full the debt he owed his master. This particular debt was for the receipt of Laban's two daughters as wives (See Gen. 29: 18, 27). Servants in that category were entitled to expect, at the completion of their period of service, that the master liberate them and send them away with a generous gift sufficient for them to provide for their immediate future. See Deut. 15:13-14.

108:6 *Jacob then tried…some old fertility tricks*: See Gen. 35:31-42. I acknowledge that my reference to 'some old fertility tricks' may appear a trifle flippant. N. Sarna states, 'Of course, this…rests on folkloristic beliefs, and fallaciously assumes the inheritability of acquired characteristics.' He goes on to note that, 'Jacob claims to have received the idea in a dream. The entire action is thus attributed to divine intervention, not to Jacob's ingenuity' (Sarna, *op. cit.*, p.212).

109:2 *The sons of Laban grew jealous*: See Gen. 31:1-21.

109:6 *That miserly hard-head*: See v.15.

110:1 *To protect him while he slept*: The Midrash suggests that Rachel acted with the best of intentions in order to wean her father off his idolatrous practice (See Rashi on v.19).

111:3 *Even using a lamp*: Our over-emphasis of the thoroughness with which

Laban searched for his idol is based on the use of the verb *mishesh* (v. 34). The special conjugation (*pi'el*) of this verb denotes particular intensiveness. Hence, the Jewish Publication Society translation renders it by 'rummaged'. See also v. 37: 'You rummaged through *all* my things'.

111:4 *She hadn't stood up*: In the biblical period, a child would stand up as a mark of respect when a parent entered, especially after the absence of some time.

112:2 *Substitution of Leah on her wedding day*: Both Rachel and Leah's aggrieved feelings towards their father, and their readiness to leave the parental home, is conveyed amid their bitter affirmation: 'Have we still a share in the inheritance of our father's house? Surely he regards us as outsiders…Whatever God has told you, you must do' (vv. 14–16).

112:3 *Never replace them…until his dying day*: See vv. 43 and 50, which, in the light of our previous note, may be rightly construed as an example of 'Laban lamely trying to cover his loss of face with empty rhetoric' (Sarna, *op.cit.*, p. 220). His pretence of deep concern for the future welfare of his daughters bears no relation to his total lack of paternal concern for their feelings up until that moment!

## Jacob and Esau's Reunion

112:5 *Especially when his scouts announced…* The Hebrew states that Jacob sent *mal'achim* to meet and pacify Esau. The precise sense of that term – which may mean either 'messenger' or 'angel' – is unclear. Following the Midrashic view (See Mid. Ber. Rabb. 75 (3)), and bearing in mind the reference to Jacob having encountered a host of 'angels of God' just previously (See Gen. 32:2), Rashi concludes that he dispatched a group of those heavenly beings to represent him to Esau.

113:1 *He might come to slay his own brother…* Setting out to justify the double expression, 'And Jacob feared greatly and was distressed' (v.8), the Midrash states that, 'He "feared greatly" that he might be killed, and "he was distressed" that he might be forced to kill others in the fray' (See Ber. Rabb. 76 (2)).

113:2 *Sending servants…express contrition*: Jacob's sense of contrition is reflected in his recurring employment of the self-abasing designation, 'your servant' each time he instructs his representatives in the precise phraseology they should use when conveying his message to Esau (See Gen. 32:5, 6, 19, 21;

33:5, 13, 15). Jacob's sense of contrition was also reflected in his exaggerated act of obeisance before Esau, bowing down to him seven times as he approaches him (See 33:3).

113:5 *He's signed treaties…to repulse a raid*: I have no biblical support for this contention, though the succession of over-generous gifts, presented by Jacob through his representatives, were clearly intended to convey the impression that he had become a very wealthy – and consequently influential – man.

114:1 Returning to retrieve arrow and quiver: The text is enigmatic, leaving unexplained the reason why Jacob, having brought his entourage over the River Jabbok, returned alone (See Gen. 32:25). The Talmud (Hullin 91a) states that he returned to collect the last few 'small receptacles,' though why they were worth all that trouble is not convincingly explained. Indeed, the previous verse states that he had already brought over the river 'everything (of value) that he possessed'. My suggestion takes account of the succeeding episode wherein he has a violent encounter with a heavenly representative of Esau. At this stage, Jacob would have wished to be well-armed in case his meeting with Esau turned violent. That he went back to retrieve his personal weapons is also supported much later when he refers to territory he seized from the Amorites 'with my sword and my bow' (Gen. 48:22).

## Wrestling with the Angel

115:1 *He begged, with arms submissively raised*: The text has the angelic adversary beg Jacob to release him, 'because day has dawned' (Gen. 32:27), though this 'explanation' remains unclear. The sages explain that, as an angel, he was charged with returning to heaven in time to sing the praise of God at dawn, especially as, on this occasion, it was his turn to lead the praise (See Tal. Hullin 91b). That angelic praise is referred to in our *Kedushah* prayer: 'We will praise your name in public in the same manner as they praise You in the highest heavens…'

115:5 *The thigh muscle of that side*: In addition to the removal, after slaughtering, of the forbidden parts of an animal, such as fats attached to the stomach and intestines (*chelev*), our dietary laws demand that the Sciatic nerve (*Gid ha-nasheh*) of the thigh be removed, as a symbolic reminder of the maiming of our father, Jacob, as described in this episode.

The act of slaughtering involves an 'onslaught' upon a lower and more vulnerable form of nature by a higher one. This exactly parallels the attack by the heavenly assailant on Jacob.

## The Jacob–Esau encounter

116:3 *Avoiding the issues that had kept them apart*: This assessment of Esau's emotional reaction is based on a literal reading of the text: 'Esau ran to meet him and embraced him; and, and, falling on his neck, he kissed him', and they (both) wept' (Gen. 33:4). Rabbinic scribal tradition insisted, however, that dots be placed above the Hebrew word *vayyishakeihu* ('he kissed him'). This was in order to take account of a Midrashic tradition that he did not kiss him wholeheartedly, since 'it is axiomatic that Esau hate*s* Jacob.' (The present continuous tense ('hates') adds a tragic and prophetic historical continuum to that hatred, with Esau symbolic of all who embrace anti-Semitism!) According to the latter assessment of Esau's action, his brotherly feelings were uncharacteristically aroused just for that moment, and he was moved to kiss Jacob (See Mid. Ber. Rabb. 78 (12)).

116:4 *On land he'd bought at the edge of the town:* See Gen. 33:18-19

## Dinah

117:1 *She preferred to wander around town alone*: This assessment of Dinah, as a free spirit with romance on her mind, accords with Midrashic tradition. It notes the opening words of this episode, 'And Dinah, *daughter of Leah*, went out' (Gen. 34:1), and links her action to that of her mother, Leah, who also 'went out' (Gen. 30:16) to meet her husband to inform him that she 'had hired him' for an extra night in exchange for the mandrakes she had given to her sister, Rachel (See Gen. 30:16 and our note on 106:2, above.). Both women had amorous adventure in mind: 'Like mother, like daughter' (Mid. Ber. Rabb. 80 (1)). It is on that basis that I introduced the theme of Dinah as frequenting the local dances, dressed in clothes that drew attention to her figure. I have actually not gone as far as the rabbis in my description. They boldly state that she followed the behaviour of her mother, Leah, who 'went out dressed provocatively, like a prostitute'.

That link, between Dinah's way of dressing and her rape, is the subject of debate in our day when, at least in Western countries, many women sport modern fashion, such as mini-skirts and décolleté tops. Some assert that this inevitably invites unwelcome (in some cases, welcome) attention, while others vehemently defend the right of people to dress as they wish, and argue, surely correctly, that no situation can justify sexual molestation and brutality. Over two thousand years, moral perceptions inevitably change. In Midrashic times, only loose women dressed provocatively, especially in the

Middle East. Hence the view of the rabbis that Dinah was the architect of her own fate.

As to the question of why Jacob deserved to be punished, and have his name besmirched, as a result of the actions of his sons, Simeon and Levi, the sages explain that this was retribution for his having hidden Dinah from Esau following their reunion. On that occasion, Jacob presents all his family to his brother, with the exception of Dinah (See Gen. 33:6-7). The Midrash suggests that, had Esau seen her, she would undoubtedly have won his heart, and she might well have turned him towards the path of repentance and righteous living. That would also have prevented Dinah's own tragic fate, for, as a married woman, she would not have fraternised with the Hittite girls (See Mid. Ber. Rabb. 76 (9)).

119:1 *One of his foes...ran to disclose*: The text does not reveal the identity of Jacob's informant (see v.5). I have conjectured that it was a local who was not too kindly disposed to his tribal leader's son, Shechem. We may assume that Dinah was not the only girl to be violated in such a manner by that tribal chieftain who wielded life and death authority. Such actions must inevitably have stirred up much silent resentment and hatred among the families of Shechem's earlier victims.

119:2 *They noted the absence of any contrition*: The absence of any contrition is clear from Hamor's opening words to Jacob's family: 'Shechem, my son, desires your daughter. Give her to him, please, as a wife' (v.8). No apology or excuse is offered for Shechem's rape of their daughter; simply a demand for them to release her as his wife.

119:4 *Enhancing our illustrious name*: See vv. 9-10.

121:3 *For those who made of our sister a whore*: The episode ends rather abruptly, with Jacob making no further response. We are left with the impression that the Torah is giving Simeon and Levi the last words, and justifying, thereby, the massacre of the Shechemites. This is especially problematic as later Sinaitic law recognises no punishment for the seduction and rape of an unmarried woman (See Deut. 22:28–29). On his deathbed, Jacob expresses once again his revulsion at his sons' action (See Gen. 49:5–7).

We are told nothing further about the life of Dinah, other than that she was among the family of Jacob that originally settled in Egypt (See Gen. 46:15). Reading between the lines of the various references to Dinah's defilement (vv. 5, 13, 27), an act described as 'an abomination' (v.7), and taken together with this final utterance of the brothers, we may assume that she was regarded as a fallen woman, defiled by idolaters, and that she probably lived out her life in disgrace and solitude.

## Death of Rachel

123:1 *Would secure an end to Israel's woes:* We allude here to the rabbinic view that Rachel's premature death was not purposeless. She was destined to be buried 'on the way to Ephrat, that is Bethlehem' (v.19), which was the highway along which the Israelites were driven into the Babylonian exile. The brevity of that exile (586–537 BCE) was perceived as having been a response to the tears shed and the prayers uttered for her children by the righteous Rachel.

According to the sages, Rachel had readily surrendered her own prospects for happiness so that her sister, Leah, might not suffer humiliation when brought to the bridal bed (See our note, above, on 73:3). Once again she is called upon to demonstrate the martyr's spirit, by surrendering up her life prematurely in order to be buried strategically on the road to Bethlehem where, in the future, she might view her offspring's plight, and offer a plaintive plea to God that He might reverse His harsh decree. This rabbinic explanation of events was inspired by the words of the prophet Jeremiah, 'The sound was heard in Ramah, weeping and bitter lamentation, Rachel crying for her children' (Jer. 31:5). R. Jacob Culi explains that it was for that reason that Jacob built a pillar, or headstone over her grave (See v.20), so that the exiles would know precisely the location of her grave and flock to it to petition for her intercession that their exile might be a short one.

## Reuben and Bilhah

123:4 *He lay with Bilhah...and thus became her man:* 'It is apparent, from several biblical stories and from ancient Near Eastern texts, that, in matters of leadership, possession of the concubine(s) of one's father or of one's vanquished enemy...bestowed legitimacy on the assumption of heirship and validated the succession...That is why King Solomon in I Kings 2:13-25 could interpret the request of [his brother] Adonijah for Abishag [his father David's concubine] as proof of treasonable intention' (N Sarna, *op. cit.*, pp. 244–245).

Reuben, although the firstborn by right of birth, yet clearly had reason to suspect that forces were at work which were seeking to displace him. First, there was his father's deepening bond with Bilhah after the death of his first wife, Rachel. Secondly, there was his father's special love for Joseph, and the latter's dreams and pretensions to leadership.

Reuben thus saw his own demotion as a looming possibility. His seizure of Bilhah, we have suggested, was an attempt to forestall such an attempt, at least from one direction.

125:1 *He'd far greater belief:* The source for our final two stanzas is the first book of Chronicles 5:1, where it states that, 'Reuben was the firstborn of Israel, but when he defiled his father's couch, his right of firstborn was transferred to the sons of Joseph, son of Israel.'

## Joseph

125:4 *And imbibe father's wisdom:* This is based on the description of Joseph as *ben zekunim* (literally, 'a son of his old age') in v.3. The authoritative Aramaic translation, Targum Onkelos, renders the phrase as 'a wise son,' adding that, 'all that Jacob had learned from Shem and Eber (See our note to 81:4, above) he transmitted to Joseph.'

125:5 *With a beauty most rare:* See Gen. 39:6.

*His stature...and his graceful gait:* In Jacob's death-bed blessing of Joseph (Gen. 49:22), he states, *banot tza'adah alei shur.* While the translations generally render it as '(Joseph is a fruitful vine) whose branches run over the wall,' the Midrash understood the word *banot* in its regular sense of 'daughters'. It thus renders the phrase, 'The daughters (of the Egyptian royalty) ran over (the palace) walls' – to catch a glimpse of him' (See Rashi on Gen. 49:22).

*And his robes well-cut, ornate:* Joseph's sartorial taste would explain why his father chose to give him 'a coat of many colours' as a mark of his love and his gratitude for Joseph's devoted care. Some view this coat as a robe of high office, the sort that would be worn by the leader of a clan on special occasions. By conferring it on Joseph he was indicating, perhaps prophetically, that this son was marked out for leadership (See also our note on 126:4, below).

126:2 *There'd be a double portion for Joseph to divide:* The double portion of the tribal inheritance was earmarked exclusively for the firstborn in early Israelite tradition. This was later codified in the law of Deuteronomy 21:17. By creating two tribes out of Joseph – those of Ephraim and Manasseh (See Deut. 48:5) – Jacob was effectively treating Joseph, his favourite son of his favourite wife, as a firstborn.

*As recompense…for all she'd been denied*: Although this is nowhere suggested, I have inferred this from the fact that, immediately after Jacob confers the double tribal privilege on Ephraim and Manasseh (Gen. 48:5-6), he speaks about the death of his beloved Rachel and how he had to bury her in the open country (v.7).

126:3 *With power to divine…heaven's plan in any situation*: After Joseph relates his dreams to his family, the Torah states, 'His brothers were jealous of him, but his father *waited on the matter*' (Gen. 37:11). Rashi explains this vague phrase to mean, 'He waited expectantly for its fulfilment.' Jacob had no doubt that God had singled out this son for some momentous purpose.

126:4 *With a coat of many colours*: There is considerable doubt as to the precise meaning of the Hebrew – *ketonet passim*. One of the main Aramaic translations, the Targum Yerushalmi, understands it as 'an embroidered cloak'. The Talmud renders it, 'a cloak of fine wool,' adding the ironic comment that 'a man should never show preference for any of his children, for, as a result of two metres of fine wool that he gave to Joseph, fate conspired to cause (Joseph to be sold and) our ancestors to have to go down to Egypt (Tal. Shabb. 10b). Another interpretation, based on the meaning of the core element of the word *passim*, namely *pas*, 'the palm of the hand,' understands the phrase as 'a garment with a long wide sleeve reaching down to the palm of the hand.' The Midrash also suggests that, being made of a silky and light material, it could be folded and compressed to be contained within 'the palm of the hand' (See Mid. Ber. Rabb 84 (8)).

127:3 *With pecuniary worth*: This is a reference to the sale of the birthright for the 'mess of pottage', or cooked lentils.

## Kidnapping and sale of Joseph

129:3 *Of regional battles brewing*: One of the major problems of this episode is why it was that, knowing of the antipathy of the other brothers toward Joseph, Jacob should have gone ahead and dispatched his beloved son into the lion's den! It has been suggested that, notwithstanding their hostility, Jacob never dreamt that they would actually resort to violence. After all, there had been family precedents for such sibling hostility, as between his father, Isaac, and his uncle Ishmael, and, even more dangerously, his own struggle with his brother, Esau. But neither of those situations had resulted in assault, violence or kidnapping! The difficulty of that explanation is that, having witnessed the savage revenge that Simeon and Levi took on the, largely innocent, inhabitants of Shechem after the rape of Dinah, Jacob should have been under no illusions as to the capacity of some of his sons for violence once their anger was aroused.

There is no doubt that Jacob would not have endangered his beloved son's life had he entertained even the slightest apprehension that his other sons intended violence against him. We are forced to re-visit, therefore, his reaction to Joseph's dreams and the bitter jealousy that they aroused among the brothers. We are told that 'his father waited (expectantly) on the matter' (Gen. 37:11. See also our note on 126:3, above). In other words, Jacob was so totally convinced that the dreams were divine revelations and portents of Joseph's future greatness that he simply could not entertain for an instant any thought that his life could be put in danger. God would protect him to ensure that His purpose was fulfilled. (It was only later, when the evidence of Joseph's torn coat seemed overwhelming, that he faced up to the fact that maybe his faith in the dreams had been a delusion. Rashi, however, explains Jacob's refusal to be comforted for the loss of his son (Gen. 37:35) on the basis of his belief that comfort was not in order since his son could not possibly have died before fulfilling his God-given mission! (See Rashi ad loc.). We have not followed Rashi's view, preferring to understand Jacob's refusal as representing a depth of grief that was too profound to be dispelled).

This may also explain why, in the wake of the Dinah episode, and Jacob's expressed realisation of the Shechemites' bitter antipathy towards his family, and desire for murderous retaliation (See Gen. 34:30), he was yet prepared to send Joseph roaming around their hostile territory in search of his brothers. In other circumstances this would have been doubly reckless!

A further reason for Jacob's action takes into account the fact that the Shechemites had been devastated and disarmed by the onslaught of Jacob's family. It is conceivable, therefore, that it was for that reason that the brothers led their sheep to pasture at Shechem, without any fear of a revenge attack. For that very reason, I suggest, Jacob had no fears about sending Joseph to wander around their territory in search of the brothers.

However, although no Shechemite posed any danger, it is probable that contending surrounding tribes would have set their sights on acquiring that now vulnerable territory. That is the force of my reference to 'regional battles brewing,' and explains Jacob's concern for his sons, tending their sheep in an area of political and military unrest. This might also explain why Jacob tells Joseph 'to go and determine *the peace of* (shelom) your brothers and their sheep.'

He was anxious to know whether his brothers had managed to maintain their *shalom* (passive state), or had become embroiled in the conflict for possession of the Shechemite lands. Having been the one's responsible for neutralising the power of that tribe, they may well have decided to press home their claim to take over its land.

130:3 *To grandpa Isaac's funeral that very day*: We have departed here from the rabbinic tradition which assumed that Isaac was still alive at this point. On the verse, 'And he (Jacob) refused to be comforted…and his father wept for him' (Gen. 37:35), the Midrash states that this refers to *Jacob's* father who wept at his son's grief (Mid. Ber. Rabb. 84 (19) ). However, bearing in mind that there is not a single specific mention of Isaac anywhere in this entire narrative and afterwards, and that his death is mentioned two chapters before the Joseph story (See Gen. 35:29; but see Rashi ad loc), we have preferred to accept another Midrashic tradition that for a long time Isaac was 'house-bound and almost like a corpse' ( See Mid. Tanh., Toldot, ch. 7. See Rashi on Gen. 38:13). Hence our line, *For years immune to those around*: We have also assumed that the Torah would hardly have introduced a reference to Isaac so much later, at the mourning for Joseph, in such a vague manner and without mentioning his name, especially as all other references to 'his father' point unambiguously to Jacob.

130:6 *Perhaps he'll forgive my shortcoming*: A reference to his having taken Bilhah, his father's concubine (See Gen.35:22), or − as the rabbis preferred to understand the text − his having removed his father's bed out of Bilhah's tent (where it had been placed after the death of his beloved, Rachel) into that of his mother, Leah (See Rashi ad loc.).

*And restore my rank somehow*: Whether or not we are doing Reuben a disservice in suggesting personal motives for his concern for Joseph, the Midrash points in that direction when it states, 'Reuben said: "I am the firstborn, and any blame will be directed at me"' (Mid. Ber. Rabb. 84 (14).

131:2 *They threw him into the empty pit*: The Torah states that, 'the pit was empty; there was no water in it' (v.24). The rabbis state, 'Isn't it obvious that, if the pit was empty, then 'there was no water in it'?! But, the implication of the latter phrase is that, 'although there was no water in it, there were other things, such as snakes and scorpions' (Tal. Shabb. 22a, and Rashi ad loc.).

*Ignoring all his pleadings*: Although the text makes no reference to Joseph's pleading − or to any other reaction on his part − the brothers later express their remorse that 'we saw the anguish of his soul when he pleaded with us, and we paid no heed' (Gen. 42:21).

131:4 *No money will accrue:* This follows the rendering of Targum Onkelos on the phrase *mah betza,* 'What will we gain?' (v.26).

132:2 *And a calculated lie:* According to the Midrash, the brothers bound each other, under a vow of excommunication, never to divulge what they had done to Joseph. Judah is credited with having taken the initiative in this. He pointed out that, because Reuben was absent, and a vow of excommunication required a minimum of ten people to confirm it, they would require to designate God as the tenth partner. Hence God was prevented from divulging the situation to Jacob! (See Mid. Tanch., ch. 2).

132:3 *The messengers that they sent:* That they dispatched messengers is implied in the phrase, 'And they *sent* the coat of many colours' (v.32). Targum Yonatan states that the chief sons sent the sons of the handmaids to perform that unsavoury task!

## Judah and Tamar

133:2 *Our consciences would now be clear:* Rashi (on Gen. 38:1) states that the other brothers condemned Judah for recommending that Joseph be sold (Gen. 37:26–27). They alleged that, with his position and great influence in the family, had he insisted that they return Joseph to his father, they would have instantly complied.

133:3 *Hurt by their…self-righteous allegation:* According to this interpretation there is a significant point of reference later in the text. The brothers' attitude to Judah we have described as 'self-righteous'. They expected Judah to have been more righteous than them, and to have prevented the injustice to Joseph. In the present episode, however, Judah publicly admits that Tamar is 'more righteous than me' (v.26). For all those years, Judah had publicly perpetrated an injustice against her, which she had borne with silent resignation. The brothers' high expectation of Judah is thus shown to have been naïve and misguided. On his own admission, even Tamar was 'more righteous' than him. The brothers' assessment of a sibling's character was shown to have been deeply flawed.

*Judah…upped and left:* See v.1: 'And it came to pass at that time that Judah *went down* from among his brethren'. Rashi (on v.1), basing himself on a statement in the Zohar, understands the text figuratively, namely that Judah was 'demoted' by his brothers. He became the scapegoat for their guilt at witnessing the grief of their father.

133:4 *He married a girl there*: Although both the biblical text and our poem present it as a marriage, it is strange that the Torah does not employ the usual term for marriage, *lakach l'ishah*, 'to take *to wife*.' Instead it states that 'he saw there (in Adulam) a Canaanite woman, and he took her and went in to her' (v.2). This is the identical phraseology used of taking a harlot or raping (*taking by force*) a woman. Ironically, it is also used later to describe Judah's action when 'he went in to' his daughter-in-law, Tamar, when she disguised herself as a harlot (vv. 16, 18). Strangely, only at her death is she described as 'Judah's' wife' (See v.12), suggestive of a situation where only later did he 'make an honest woman of her!' By contrast the word 'wife' is clearly employed at the outset in reference to the partners of his sons (See vv. 6, 8, 9). Is the Torah offering us here a rationale for Judah's later exposure? Having 'taken' a woman from the idolatrous and degenerate Canaanite tribe – for which reason he may have been disinclined to marry her – his own two older sons display a similar 'Canaanite morality' (See Lev. 18:3) in their intimate relations with their wives (See Gen. 38:7, 9-10).

134:1 *To take his late brother's wife*: The reference here is to what is called 'levirate marriage', from the Latin, *levir*, 'a husband's brother.' When a brother dies without heir, the surviving brother is duty-bound to marry the widow (See Deut. 25:5).

134:2 *Reducing his own parental pride*: We may find it rather difficult to understand why Onan should have been concerned that any child born from his levirate union with Tamar might grow up owing emotional loyalty to the memory of his late 'father'. Surely the child's allegiance would be exclusively to his biological father! This calls into question the meaning of the Torah's rationale of the levirate institution, namely, 'to perpetuate the memory of the deceased' (Deut. 25:6).

We can only assume that it was the mother's responsibility constantly to remind the child that, unlike other women, who, at the death of their husbands, were free to chose whomsoever they desired as a second husband, in her case, that choice was removed. Her second marriage to his father, the *levir*, was, imposed, as a symbolic commemoration of a life cut short and 'love's labours lost'. The message she would have been expected to convey to the child was that, in addition to his love and respect for his natural father (and herself), he was to attempt to bring an extra measure of pride to the family, through a life of piety and service, so that people would have cause to praise him, and, in so doing, to mention his parents. By association, they would inevitably recall the qualities of the deceased – 'the father that never was'. The wicked Onan was clearly not prepared to have the shadow of his departed older brother cast over him in that way. He may also have set his heart on taking a virgin to wife, and was not prepared, therefore, to have his late brother's wife forced upon him by local convention. It was not until centuries later that Deuteronomic law enabled the *levir* to avoid such an imposition by undergoing the ritual of *chalitzah* (See Dt. 25:7).

135:1 *Even later, after Judah's wife died*: See Gen. 38:12.

135:5 *'I'll take in pledge your raiment…*  Judah was effectively pawning these items on the understanding that the harlot would return them at a later date when her customer brought her 'a kid from the flock.'

135:6 *'Give me your belt, your seals and staff*: The seal was the equivalent of our credit card. A person would have his distinctive emblem engraved on a cylinder which was often worn around the neck. Rolled over soft clay, the impression would serve to 'seal' and validate, or identify, documents.

136:3 *'A wife in waiting! A heinous crime'*: Tamar's marital status is described in later rabbinic law as that of *shomeret yavam*, 'one awaiting the union with the *levir*.' As with the betrothed maiden 'awaiting a husband,' the former was also expected to maintain the sexual loyalty of a full wife, albeit that the full relationship had not yet been finalised. Any extra-marital liaison was thus regarded as an act of adultery (See Lev. 20:10).

## Joseph in Egypt

137:3 *Joseph's beauty was the talk of the court*: The ancient sages, ever concerned to understand why trials are imposed upon the righteous, concluded that Joseph must have been responsible in some way for the wife of Potiphar's attempt at his seduction. On the verse, 'Joseph was endowed with a fine physique and a beautiful appearance' (Gen. 39:6), the Midrash states that, 'when he reached a position of authority he began to be fastidious with his diet and to curl his hair. God thereupon said: 'Your father is in mourning for you, and you are only concerned with your appearance! I shall let loose against you, therefore, a dangerous bear.' This explains the following verse: 'And the wife of his master…said, "Lie with me"' (Mid. Ber. Rabb. 87 (12), and Rashi on Gen. 39:6.'

138:1 *'Lie with me, one day she pleaded.* N. Sarna appositely points out that 'there are no verbal preliminaries, no expression of love. Her peremptory mode of speech flows from her consciousness of Joseph's status as a slave. In no other biblical narrative does a woman brazenly proposition a man in this manner' (*JPS Torah Commentary*, p.273).

138:2 *Day after day Joseph resisted*: Midrash Tanchuma states that she amorously pursued Joseph for an entire year (See on Vayyeshev, ch.8).

138:3 *While pointing at Joseph a finger of blame*: On the verse, 'And it was that one day he came into the house [of Potiphar] to do his work, with none of the men of the house present there' (Gen. 39:11), the Midrash states that his intention that day was to succumb to Potiphar's wife's desire. However, at that moment he had a vision of his father's face, and he desisted (See Mid. Ber. Rabb. 87 (9) and Rashi on Gen. 39:11).

139:3 *Who whispered it around for their own ends!*: The Midrash depicts Potiphar's wife as telling all her friends just how love-sick she was for Joseph. It describes her as changing into alluring dresses three times a day in her desperate attempt to seduce him.

140:1 *He sentenced Joseph to incarceration*: Had Potiphar truly believed his wife's allegation, there is no doubt that he would have peremptorily executed Joseph. Hence our speculative suggestions in the above stanzas for what might have convinced him that she was not to be believed.

140:3 *Been appointed to a prison directorate!*: The Midrash states that Joseph was incarcerated for twelve years. Assuming that he was sold at eighteen, and had a further two years in Potiphar's home before being jailed, he would at this time have been thirty-two years of age.

## The Butler and the Baker

140:4 *Pharaoh's butler and baker got drunk one day*: We have employed some poetic imagination in our suggestion that the butler and baker's misdemeanours were the result of their having been drunk. We have assumed that there must have been some specific cause for those two supreme officials offending at one and the same time. Getting drunk together seems a most plausible motivation.

*While his bread, in wagon oil was smothered:* The Torah states, simply, that 'the king of Egypt's butler and baker gave offence to (literally, 'sinned against') their lord' (v.1). Rabbinic tradition fills in the details by stating that 'the king discovered a fly in his goblet and a pebble in his bread' (Mid. Ber. Rabb. 88 (1)). With poetic licence, we have slightly varied one of the details of this tradition.

142:1 *Laden with loaves, cakes and cream:* The text states, generally, 'all kinds of food…that a baker prepares' (v.17).

## Pharaoh's Dreams

143:6 *Pharaoh knew that they had lied:* This is based on Pharaoh's admission that he had consulted his magicians, but none had been able to elucidate his dreams to his satisfaction (vv.8, 24). The Midrash provides several examples of the magicians' speculative interpretations, such as that Pharaoh would beget seven daughters, and then bury them all.

The Siftei Chakhamim (commentary on Rashi) states that Pharaoh's rejection of their interpretations was intuitive, especially when he heard Joseph's elucidation of his dreams. Pharaoh had always felt that his dream was a portent of something affecting his entire nation, not a purely personal disclosure.

144:3 *When that lad revealed just what they meant:* Significantly, the butler never refers to Joseph by name, merely as 'a Hebrew lad, a slave to the Chief Steward' (v.12). Rashi views this description as an attempt by the butler to demean and depersonalise Joseph, for fear that the king might appreciate his ability and statesmanship, and elevate him (See Rashi on v.12).

## Reunion of Joseph and his Brothers

149:5 *By the addition of a beard:* This is Rashi's explanation of why the brothers did not recognise Joseph (See Rashi on v.8).

## Further trials for the Brothers

156:2 *Five rings, exquisitely wrought:* We have offered here our own interpretation of the Hebrew term *chamesh yadot* (Gen. 43:34), generally rendered, 'five portions,' that is five times what he gave to the other brothers. Since *yadot* may also be a plural form of *yad* ('hand'), an alternative to the usual dual form, *yadayim*, we have understood it as 'hand rings'. Our rendering of the entire v.34 would then be, 'Gifts were proffered to them all by him, but Benjamin's gift was much greater than all of theirs, namely five rings.'

157:1 *And jail for the rest without trial:* See Gen. 44:9.

## Joseph discloses his identity

159:6 *Twenty wagons laden with grain:* Joseph actually divides up his cavalcade into 'ten he-asses, laden with the best of Egypt, and ten she-asses, laden with grain, bread and provisions' (Gen. 45:23). Whatever the reason for dividing up his cavalcade into two groups of ten, it evokes, unmistakably, the identical number of ten camels sent by Abraham to the home of Rebekah, bearing gifts to shower on her and her family to encourage them to allow her to leave to become Isaac's wife (Gen. 24:10), and to ensure that he, Abraham, would have a posterity, in fulfilment of God's promise.

Abraham was told by God that his offspring would one day be enslaved in a foreign land for a long period before achieving their independence. The ten wagons he sent represented the first of three stages in the ultimate realisation of God's promise: national expansion (through marriage and procreation), enslavement, and redemption. This lends added significance to the fact that, when the brothers returned and told Jacob that Joseph was still alive and ruling over Egypt, 'he did not believe them' (Gen. 45:26). It was only 'when he saw the wagons that Joseph had sent to transport him' that 'the spirit of their father, Jacob, was lifted' (v.27).

It was only when Jacob saw the double cavalcade, each of ten wagons, that he became convinced that God's plan was now in motion. His son, Joseph, the foretold agent of that redemption, simply had still to be alive. Destiny was beckoning!

## Jacob's Last Days

163:1 *For seventeen years*: Like father like son: Joseph was seventeen years of age when he had his dreams foretelling his rise to leadership, and his father enjoyed seventeen years of benefit of the fruit of that leadership.

## The Brothers' apprehension

170:2 *So an intercessor was sent to speak:* We have here an echo of the intercessors sent by their father, Jacob, to his brother, Esau, when the former had been unable to ascertain his brother's attitude towards him. This is an example of the rabbinic maxim, *Ma'asei avot siman lebanim*, 'the actions of the fathers foreshadow those of their offspring'.